ROMEO & JULIET

THE 1-HOUR GUIDEBOOK

AN ILLUSTRATED GUIDE FOR MASTERING SHAKESPEARE'S GREATEST LOVE STORY

David Grey & Gigi Bach, editors

SPARK NOTES

A Division of Barnes & Noble Publishing

This edition published by Spark Educational Publishing in agreement with Bermond Press.

SPARKNOTES is a registered trademark of SparkNotes LLC.

Spark Educational Publishing
A Division of Barnes & Noble Publishing
120 Fifth Avenue
New York, NY 10011

Printed in the United States of America

10 9 8 7 6 5 4 3 2 1

ISBN 1-4114-0447-5
Library of Congress Catalog-in-Publication Data available on request.

Cover and book design by Dreamedia, Inc.

NEW & UPCOMING TITLES

IN THE 1-HOUR GUIDEBOOK SERIES

Hamlet
Romeo & Juliet
Macbeth
Julius Caesar
A Midsummer Night's Dream
Othello

CONTENTS

ACKNOWLEDGEMENTS

The editors would like to extend our warmest gratitude to the following people who supported us with their encouragement, feedback, proofreading and inspiration: Barbara, David and Beverly, Lisa, Brian, Professor Louis A. Montrose and Professor Harold Bloom.

FOREWORD

This book emerged from our desire to provide the unfamiliar reader with the most comprehensive, clear picture of Shakespeare's *Romeo and Juliet* in the least amount of time. In addition, our awe of Shakespeare's masterpiece nurtured a passion to present the information in a way that complemented the greatness of his work. Why shouldn't the beauty of a Shakespeare primer at least attempt to mirror the beauty of the subject? Briefly stated, why does a literary guidebook have to look ugly? The obvious answer is that it doesn't, especially when illustration collaborating with text is the best way to accomplish our desire for clarity and quick assimilation. Neither text nor graphics is exclusive to the brain. We think in pictures; we think in words. The cognitive interaction between the two is the quickest path to understanding.

When developing a picture of our audience, therefore, we held these characteristics foremost: frightening lack of time, need for clarity, desire for beauty.

Certain innovations arose in attempting to satisfy this model—visual distillations, plot timelines, dramatic maps, quick reviews of the characters, scene by scene illustrations and more. By the same criteria, certain traditional elements were eliminated—you won't, for example, find lengthy commentary in this book. Most of the commentary we have found in other study guides to Shakespeare was either overly obvious or arguably incorrect. To take up valuable time with our own commentary would be counter to our purpose, which we felt demanded concrete summary rather than questionable surmise.

As far as our specific decisions regarding *Romeo and Juliet,* at every opportunity we tried to convey some sense of the desperate emotionality unique to Shakespeare's rendition. We tried to trace this powerful thread of emotionality from its onset with the Pilgrim sonnet, through the play's most significant moments—the voluptuous balcony meeting, the tense Epithalamium, the heart-rending Aubade—

until its fulfillment with the double-suicide. The emotionality conveyed through these moments was certainly one of humankind's greatest experiments in the ability of language to reveal the transcendent breach that occurs when the intrinsic natural, physical, social and emotional boundaries between two people collapse, allowing them to become exclusively, inseparably—and, yes, dangerously—devoted to each other. The moments shared by Romeo and Juliet are still the unapproachable paragons of their genre. Any shortfall in our communicating this is, of course, no fault of the playright's.

We adopted a naming convention of lower-cased titles, such as "the prince," unless they were proper nouns ("Prince Escalus"). One major exception is that of the Nurse, which we capitalized throughout. As you have seen, we have also chosen to capitalize "Epithalamium" and "Aubade" when referring to the aubade and epithalamium specific to *Romeo and Juliet*; we trade the violation for the emphasis.

Our scene by scene summaries give equal, single-page weight to each scene division, except in the case of 5.3, which by sheer volume needed to be split into two parts after the suicide of Romeo, as well as six scenes which we felt could best be explained in combination: 4.2-3, 4.4-5 and 5.1-2. We ask your indulgence.

Congratulations on your adventure into Shakespeare's inimitable masterwork.

David Grey & Gigi Bach, editors

It is love, not reason, that is stronger than death.

Thomas Mann
The Magic Mountain

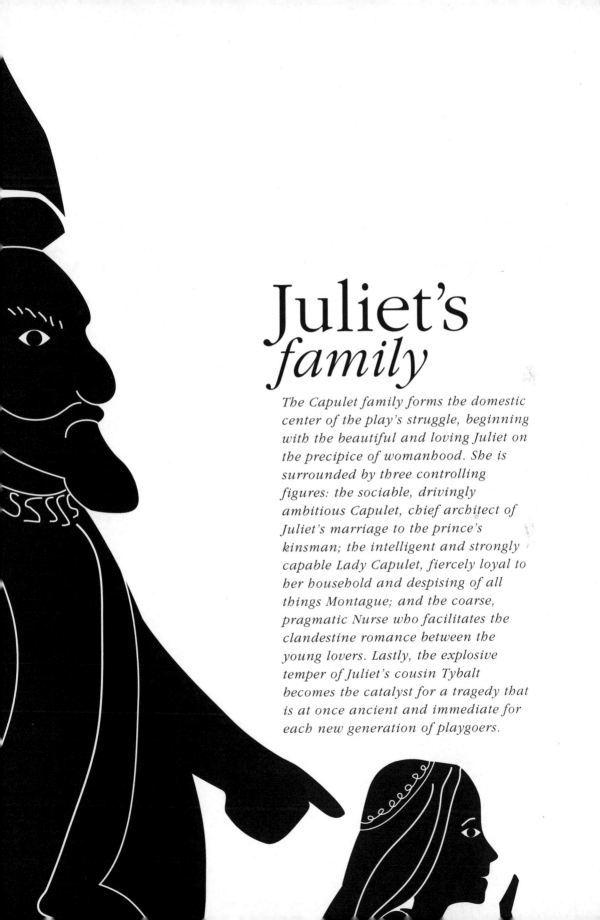

Juliet's
family

The Capulet family forms the domestic
center of the play's struggle, beginning
with the beautiful and loving Juliet on
the precipice of womanhood. She is
surrounded by three controlling
figures: the sociable, drivingly
ambitious Capulet, chief architect of
Juliet's marriage to the prince's
kinsman; the intelligent and strongly
capable Lady Capulet, fiercely loyal to
her household and despising of all
things Montague; and the coarse,
pragmatic Nurse who facilitates the
clandestine romance between the
young lovers. Lastly, the explosive
temper of Juliet's cousin Tybalt
becomes the catalyst for a tragedy that
is at once ancient and immediate for
each new generation of playgoers.

MY ONLY LOVE

sprung from my only hate,
too early seen unknown and known too late.
Prodigious birth of love it is to me
That I must love a loathéd enemy.

1.5.140-143

THIS IS
JULIET

JULIET IS A YOUNG GIRL two weeks short of her fourteenth birthday. She comes from a wealthy family called the Capulets, living in Verona, Italy.

Her circle of contacts is small, consisting of only her mother, father, nurse and priest. She is nearly always seen indoors, either alone or with only one or two others. This tight circle exerts a great deal of control over her, but as we shall see, she soon breaks free of all control in a most dramatic way. Juliet and her true love Romeo are the central characters in the play.

TAKE
ALL MYSELF

Although she has led a sheltered life, early on we see Juliet responding to Romeo's advances like a woman well beyond her years. She is intelligent and witty in her dealings with her elders, confounding the Nurse and fooling her parents. She is described in famous terms as possessing beauty and sweetness. Her utterances in the play are unmatched in sublimity by any other character, which makes her an all the more tragic figure.

SIBLINGS
Juliet may be the only surviving child of the Capulets. Her nurse mentions Susan, a girl who died young and was the same age as Juliet. It is unclear whether Susan was Juliet's twin or the Nurse's own child.

SUN
In what is probably the most familiar scene in all literature, Romeo sees Juliet at her balcony and declares that her beauty is the sun itself. The sun symbol on the opposite page will be our shorthand symbol for Juliet.

TYBALT, MY COUSIN!

O my brother's child!
O prince! O cousin! Husband! O, the blood is spilt.
O my dear kinsman! Prince, as thou art true,
For blood of ours, shed blood of Montague.

3.1.150-153

QUESTION
Juliet hails from what aristocratic family in Verona? (ANSWER ON PAGE 18)

JULIET HAS A
MOTHER

SHE IS LADY CAPULET,
the intelligent, calculating
wife of Lord Capulet. She
is concerned for Juliet's
well being, but only so far
as that well being furthers
the prosperity of the
Capulet family.

Lady Capulet forms a powerfully
logical complement to her husband's
gregarious emotionality. Together,
they head up one of the two most
successful aristocratic families in
Verona. While loyal to her
husband, Lady Capulet is
anything but subservient, forming
a circle of some independence
with the Nurse and Juliet.
When Juliet's father is
negotiating her marriage, it is
Lady Capulet who acts as
liaison between them.

PROTOTYPE
In 1.3 Lady Capulet tells
Juliet to begin thinking
of marriage, since she
herself was very near to
Juliet's age when she
became a mother. Statements
such as these help normalize
to the audience Juliet's
marriageability at such
a young age.

WE WILL
HAVE VENGEANCE FOR IT

Sadly, Lady Capulet's extreme rationality
blocks her awareness of her daughter's
true feelings. Thus, when Romeo kills
Lady Capulet's nephew Tybalt, it is she
who calls for vengeance, which ultimately
results in Romeo's banishment and her
own daughter's death.

I DO NOT USE TO JEST.

Thursday is near; lay hand on heart, advise:
An you be mine, I'll give you to my friend;
And you be not, hang, beg, starve, die in the streets,
For by my soul, I'll never acknowledge thee,
Nor what is mine shall never do thee good:
trust to't, bethink you; I'll not be forsworn.

3.5.199-206

ANSWER
Juliet is a Capulet.

QUESTION
What is the reason Lady Capulet wants Romeo killed? (ANSWER ON PAGE 20)

SHE ALSO HAS A
FATHER

HE IS REFERRED TO BY his surname, Capulet, and he is a wealthy aristocrat of Verona. Capulet is defined by a gregarious extroversion, coupled with driving ambition.

The outward sign of his ambition in the play is his fateful negotiation of Juliet's hand in marriage to Paris, kinsman to the prince. With this marriage, Capulet hopes to further his family's status.

I THINK
SHE WILL BE RULED

When Capulet discovers that Juliet is not happy with the arranged marriage, he becomes short-tempered and unreasonable. He threatens to disown her if she does not submit to his choice of a husband for her. Juliet then feigns submission, but follows through with a dubious strategy, which ends in tragedy for all involved.

BUSINESSMAN

Capulet is very concerned with preserving his legacy: Juliet is his only child and he thus wishes to guarantee her financial security while strengthening political alliances. Paris, kinsman to the prince, fits both bills nicely. Since he is so commercially motivated, our shorthand symbol for Capulet will be a bag of gold.

TOLERANCE

After the opening civil disturbance, Capulet is painted as a fair and tolerant man. He expresses the need for Paris to win Juliet's affection before he can approve of their marriage. He also tolerates Romeo's presence at the feast. This picture is a vivid contrast to his mean-spirited threats to Juliet in 3.5.

HIE TO YOUR CHAMBER:

I'll find Romeo
To comfort you: I wot well where he is.
Hark ye, your Romeo will be here tonight:
I'll to him; he is hid at Lawrence's cell.

3.2.142-145

THIS IS JULIET's
NURSE

SHE IS ALSO JULIET'S closest friend and confidant, having raised Juliet since she was an infant. Since the Nurse's husband is now dead, she lives at the Capulet house with Juliet.

Besides Friar Lawrence, the Nurse is the only adult who knows of Romeo and Juliet's love. She brings word from Romeo to Juliet concerning the details of their elopement; she carries with her the rope ladder Romeo uses to enter Juliet's room on their wedding night; she tells Juliet of Romeo's banishment to Mantua.

SEEK
HAPPY NIGHTS

After Capulet decrees that Juliet must marry Paris, Juliet begs the Nurse for advice. The Nurse answers that Juliet must abandon her dreams of Romeo (after all, he has been banished) and be happy to marry Paris, who the Nurse believes is a better man. This is the turning point in the Nurse and Juliet's relationship. From that moment, Juliet acts alone—without support from her lifelong friend.

BAWDY
The defining characteristic of the Nurse is her insatiable desire to engage in bawdy humor. Her low-comic sexuality is a burlesque parody of the pure, heartfelt and sublime love embodied by Juliet.

CONTROL
Along with Lord and Lady Capulet, the Nurse completes the triplet of controlling figures in Juliet's life. Our shorthand symbol for the Nurse will be a ladybird—or ladybug—a term of endearment she first uses to call Juliet.

THIS, BY HIS VOICE,

should be a Montague.
Fetch me my rapier, boy. What, dares the slave
Come hither, cover'd with an antic face,
To fleer and scorn at our solemnity?
Now, by the stock and honor of my kin,
To strike him dead, I hold it not a sin.

1.5.56-61

ANSWER
Capulet arranges for his daughter to marry Paris, kinsman of the prince.

QUESTION
Who functions as a liaison between Juliet and Romeo? (ANSWER ON PAGE 25)

THIS IS JULIET's
COUSIN

HIS NAME IS TYBALT and he is the only male Capulet heir, the son of Lady Capulet's brother. A gentleman, Tybalt is well-educated and schooled in fencing.

He is, however, an uncontrollable hothead. Hearing Romeo's voice at the Capulet feast, Tybalt tells his page to fetch his sword. Capulet overhears him and frustrates Tybalt's disruption of Juliet's cotillion. Later, Tybalt sends Romeo a letter of challenge.

YOU ARE
A SAUCY BOY

When Tybalt comes looking for Romeo in the square, Mercutio—equally volatile—insults him and goads him into a swordfight. Romeo tries to break it up and Tybalt stabs Mercutio beneath Romeo's arm, killing him. Romeo then kills Tybalt, resulting in his banishment by the prince.

GRIEF
Juliet grieves at the news of Romeo's banishment, sobbing day and night. Her mother and father believe, however, that she is mourning the untimely death of her cousin Tybalt at the hand of a Montague.

HAUNTING
Just before she drinks the sleeping potion, Juliet hallucinates that she sees the ghost of Tybalt, searching for Romeo. She calls for him to stop and then drinks the potion down. Later in Juliet's tomb, Romeo spots the dead body of Tybalt and asks his forgiveness before killing himself.

A SUMMARY of JULIET's FAMILY

mother

father

Lady Capulet
ARISTOCRAT OF VERONA

Juliet's mother. Wife of Capulet and aunt to Tybalt. She is intelligent, logical and fiercely loyal to the Capulet family. With Juliet and the Nurse, she forms a circle of some independence. During the marriage negotiations with Paris, she acts as liaison between Juliet and Capulet. After her nephew Tybalt is slain by Romeo, she demands the prince put Romeo to death. The sentence is commuted to banishment.

Capulet
ARISTOCRAT OF VERONA

Juliet's father. Husband of Lady Capulet. Wealthy head of the Capulet family. He is gregarious and ambitious. Concerned with preserving his legacy, he negotiates Juliet's marriage to Paris, kinsman to the prince. Initially well-meaning and tolerant, he becomes unreasonably angry and threatens to disown Juliet. It is Capulet who organizes Juliet's cotillion—the famous Capulet feast— where Romeo and Juliet first meet.

arm of strength

bag of gold

The Nurse

JULIET'S CHILDHOOD NANNY

Bawdy childhood nanny to Juliet. Friend and closest confidant among Juliet's family. She is the only adult—other than the friar—who knows of Romeo and Juliet's clandestine love. The Nurse acts as liaison between the young lovers: arranging meetings, carrying the rope ladder Romeo uses to enter Juliet's bedroom, bringing news of Romeo's crime and banishment. At play's end, she pragmatically recommends Juliet abandon her dreams of Romeo, causing Juliet to hate her.

ladybird

Tybalt

MALE CAPULET HEIR

Juliet's hotheaded cousin. Lady Capulet's nephew (her brother's son). Well educated. Schooled in fencing. Incensed at seeing Romeo at the Capulet feast, he later sends him a formal challenge. Romeo declines, but Mercutio takes his place and is killed when Romeo steps between them. Enraged, Romeo kills Tybalt, bringing his own banishment. Juliet sees Tybalt's ghost before drinking the friar's sleeping potion.

sword

ANSWER The Nurse acts as liaison between Juliet and Romeo.

Romeo's *family*

The Montagues of Verona function less as a domestic entity than as a rival house to the Capulets. For example, Lord Montague is shown less as a parent—although he does worry about Romeo's reclusive moodiness—than as a ready combatant in the feud's first violence or as a grandstanding penitent in the final reconciliation scene. Romeo's cousin, Benvolio, exhibits an undaunted pacifism that is a breath of fresh air within the grotesque hostility that permeates all strata of the city. Friar Lawrence, though not a Montague, is Romeo's chief counselor, having advised him through at least his brief infatuation with Rosaline. It is he who tries to usher the lovers into the adult world: his good intentions unwittingly orchestrating their fateful end.

BUT SOFT,

What light through yonder window breaks?
It is the east, and Juliet is the sun.
Arise, fair sun, and kill the envious moon,
Who is already sick and pale with grief,
That thou her maid art far more fair than she:
Be not her maid, since she is envious;
Her vestal livery is but sick and green
And none but fools do wear it; cast it off.
It is my lady, O, it is my love!
O, that she knew she were!

2.2.2-11

QUESTION
Who kills Juliet's cousin Tybalt? (ANSWER ON PAGE 30)

THIS IS JULIET's
TRUE LOVE

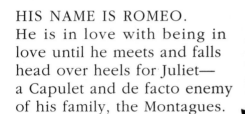

HIS NAME IS ROMEO.
He is in love with being in
love until he meets and falls
head over heels for Juliet—
a Capulet and de facto enemy
of his family, the Montagues.

Romeo first sees Juliet at her
cotillion, a feast organized by
her father. They share their
first kiss only to discover
their surnames at party's
end. That evening, Romeo
speaks with Juliet from
beneath her balcony
and they declare their
mutual love. Afterward,
Romeo visits Friar
Lawrence, his spiritual
advisor, and convinces him
to secretly marry them.

I AM
FORTUNE'S FOOL

What follows is a cascade of
youthful decisions that consumes
their brief relationship with its
own passion. The afternoon of
his wedding, Romeo is challenged
by Tybalt in the public square. He
refuses to fight, but Romeo's friend
Mercutio is killed when he takes Romeo's
place. Enraged, Romeo kills Tybalt and is
banished. Hearing misguided news that
Juliet is dead (she stages her death to
remain faithful to Romeo), Romeo returns
to Verona where he drinks poison and dies.

CONTROLS
In contrast to Juliet, Romeo
is nearly always seen outdoors,
away from his home. Instead of
the tight circle of controlling adults
that smothers Juliet, Romeo is
surrounded by a controlling
social group of adolescent male
friends—headed by Mercutio—
who encourage him to act on
his sexual impulses, but not on
his emotional passions.

PILGRIM
The name "Romeo" means
"wanderer" or "pilgrim." Shakespeare
wrote Romeo and Juliet's first meeting
as a sonnet, with Romeo, a pilgrim, paying
homage to Juliet, a saint. Pilgrims were
recognized for carrying palm branches—a sign
of Christ's divinity—which will be our shorthand
symbol for Romeo.

MANY A MORNING

hath he there been seen,
With tears augmenting the fresh morning dew.
Adding to clouds more clouds with his deep sighs;
But all so soon as the all-cheering sun
Should in the furthest east begin to draw
The shady curtains from Aurora's bed,
Away from the light steals home my heavy son...

1.1.123-129

ANSWER
Romeo kills Juliet's cousin, Tybalt, after Tybalt kills Mercutio, Romeo's good friend.

QUESTION
Where do Romeo and Juliet first meet and kiss? (ANSWER ON PAGE 32)

THESE ARE ROMEO's
PARENTS

LORD AND LADY MONTAGUE. They function primarily as rivals to Lord and Lady Capulet, who they despise. When the servants cause a general riot in the opening scene, Montague rushes to join the fray, much to the consternation of his wife.

Once the fighting is over, Montague is ordered to see the prince that afternoon in an attempt to bring an end to the hostility between the two families. Lady Montague is relieved to learn that Romeo was not in the fighting.

SET THIS
ANCIENT QUARREL NEW

After the bodies of Romeo and Juliet are discovered in the tomb, Montague reveals that his wife has died from grief over Romeo's banishment. Capulet offers Montague a truce and Montague accepts, saying he will erect a priceless, solid gold statue of Juliet in Verona.

MOUNTAIN
The surname Montague means "steep mountain," which will be our shorthand symbol for Romeo's parents.

...YOU SAW HER FAIR,

none else being by,
Herself poised with herself in either eye:
But in that crystal scales let there be weigh'd
Your lady's love against some other maid
That I will show you shining at this feast,
And she shall scant show well that now shows best.

1.2.96-101

ANSWER
Romeo and Juliet first meet and kiss at the Capulet feast.

QUESTION
What does the name "Montague" mean? (ANSWER ON PAGE 34)

THIS IS ROMEO's
COUSIN

HIS NAME IS BENVOLIO.
In contrast to most of his
peers, Benvolio is a lover of
peace. In fact, we first see him
attempting to diffuse the
servants' quarrel in the
opening scene of the play.

Tybalt, who is
equal in status to
Benvolio, frustrates
his efforts and the
quarrel soon erupts
into a general riot.
After the prince
diffuses the violence,
Benvolio tells the
Montagues of Romeo's
reclusive behavior. When
Montague confirms that Romeo has been
depressed, Benvolio volunteers to
uncover the roots of his melancholy.

I DO BUT
KEEP THE PEACE

Benvolio finds, indeed, that Romeo
is in love with a girl—Rosaline—who does
not return his affections. He counsels his
cousin to go with him to the Capulet feast
that evening where Benvolio will show him
dozens of girls who will make him forget all
about Rosaline. Romeo agrees, but only because
he knows Rosaline will be there. Once at the
feast, however, Romeo catches sight of Juliet
and is struck by true love like a thunderbolt.

GOODHEARTED
The name "Benvolio"
suggests benevolence
and is an apt label
for Romeo's goodhearted
cousin. Our shorthand
symbol for Benvolio will
be the peace dove.

TAKE THOU THIS VIAL

being then in bed,
And this distilled liquor drink thou off;
When presently through all thy veins shall run
A cold and drowsy humor, for no pulse
Shall keep his native progress, but surcease:
No warmth, no breath, shall testify thou livest;
The roses in thy lips and cheeks shall fade
To paly ashes, thy eyes' windows fall,
Like death, when he shuts up the day of life....

4.1.94-102

ANSWER
The surname "Montague" means "steep mountain."

QUESTION
Who blocks Benvolio's attempt to diffuse the servants' quarrel in the opening scene? (ANSWER ON PAGE 37)

THIS IS ROMEO's
ADVISOR

FRIAR LAWRENCE IS THE only adult character other than the Nurse who knows of Romeo and Juliet's clandestine love. The good friar is the first person Romeo runs to after he and Juliet declare their love following the Capulet feast.

Striking a balance between a refreshing optimism and a constant exhortation to temperance, the friar agrees to marry the youngsters because he hopes it will reconcile the two feuding families.

I'LL THY
ASSISTANT BE

An amateur botanist, the friar concocts a sleeping potion for Juliet to drink which causes her to appear dead. After his strategy brings the death of the lovers, he recounts the story to the prince and the patriarchs, accepting full responsibility for the tragedy. The prince, however, recognizes the friar's good intentions and grants him full pardon.

DESPERATION
Friar Lawrence is the only one present when Juliet awakens. Hearing the watch approaching, the friar urges her to leave with him, promising to hide her among a sisterhood of nuns. Juliet declines and the friar flees, fearing he will be punished for his role in Romeo's death.

A SUMMARY *of* ROMEO's FAMILY

father and mother

Montagues
ARISTOCRATS OF VERONA

Romeo's parents are embroiled in an ancient feud with Juliet's parents, the Capulets. In fact, we see Montague fighting his rivals early in the play, after which he is called to task by the prince. Lady Montague is relieved to discover Romeo was not involved in the riot. After Romeo is banished from Verona, however, for killing Juliet's cousin Tybalt, Lady Montague dies of grief. After the tragic deaths of Romeo and Juliet, Montague vows to erect a solid gold statue of Juliet in Verona.

steep mountain

cousin   *spiritual advisor*

Benvolio
YOUNG GENTLEMAN

First seen attempting to stop the servants' quarrel in the opening scene, Benvolio is a man of peace in contrast to his peers. Early in the play, he counsels Romeo to forget his infatuation for Rosaline, who will not return his affection. He urges Romeo to accompany him to the Capulet feast where Benvolio will show him many other beauties to make him forget Rosaline. At play's end, Benvolio is the only surviving character in his peer group.

Friar Lawrence
FRIAR & AMATEUR BOTANIST

Friar Lawrence attempts—albeit clumsily—to facilitate the entry of the adolescent lovers into the adult world. He risks angering the rival patriarchs (hoping the marriage will instead end the feud), but he is ill prepared for the horrible consequences that actually occur. He is the architect of the plot to feign Juliet's death, but his fellow friar bungles the message to Romeo. He assumes responsibility for the tragedy, but receives a full pardon in the end.

dove of peace

crucifix

ANSWER Tybalt, Juliet's cousin, stops Benvolio from diffusing the servants' quarrel, drawing his sword and forcing him to fight.

the Prince's *family*

Prince Escalus represents authority at the limits of failure: aloof, unable to operate against the hostility-infused daily lives of its citizens and ultimatum-driven when it tries. Despite his displays of temperance—for which he chides himself at the end of the play—Prince Escalus is a distant, crises dependent ruler. His kinsmen, nevertheless, provide us the two least and most charismatic personalities of the play: namely, that of the laconic Paris—rational counter to the passionate Romeo—and the witty Mercutio—intellectual counter to the slow-witted Tybalt. Mercutio's death steers the play into tragedy, placing all hope for a happy ending on the Friar's dubious strategy.

REBELLIOUS SUBJECTS,

enemies to peace,
Profaners of this neighbor-stained steel—
Will they not hear? What, ho! You men, you beasts,
That quench the fire of your pernicious rage
With purple fountains issuing from your veins,
On pain of torture, from those bloody hands
Throw your mistemper'd weapons to the ground,
And hear the sentence of your moved prince.

1.1.74-81

QUESTION
Who is the only person who sees Juliet awaken in the tomb? (ANSWER ON PAGE 42)

THIS IS THE PRINCE

PRINCE ESCALUS MAINTAINS a distant control over the city of Verona, plagued by the feuding of two of its aristocratic patriarchs—Capulet and Montague. He enters the play after a quarrel erupts into a general riot and he decrees that the next to disturb the peace will pay with their lives.

After Romeo kills Tybalt, Lady Capulet demands Prince Escalus enforce his decree. But, the prince fairly commutes the sentence to that of banishment.

YOUR
LIVES SHALL PAY

Once the bodies of Romeo, Juliet and Paris are discovered, the officers of the watch call for the prince and the patriarchs. After the prince arrives at the tomb, he gathers the facts of the situation from the testimony of Friar Lawrence and Romeo's servant, Balthazar. He scolds both Montague and Capulet and blames himself for overlooking their violence. His closing monition forms the final quatrain and couplet of a sonnet.

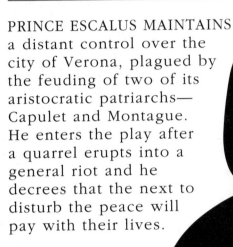

CRISES
The prince remains aloof for the main action of the play, showing up only in times of extreme crisis: the riot, the death of Tybalt and the deaths of Romeo, Juliet and Paris.

IMPORTANCE
Verona remained a strategically important European city from the the birth of the Roman empire. An aristocratic family in 1260 shaped the city into the commercial and artistic force for which it came to be known.

IF LOVE BE ROUGH

with you, be rough with love;
Prick love for pricking, and you beat love down.
Give me a case to put my visage in:
A visor for a visor! What care I
What curious eye doth quote deformities?

1.4.27-31

ANSWER
Friar Lawrence is the only person to see Juliet awaken in the tomb (Romeo and Paris are dead).

QUESTION
What is the sentence Prince Escalus gives Romeo for killing Tybalt? (ANSWER ON PAGE 44)

THIS IS ROMEO's
FRIEND

QUITE EASILY THE MOST charismatic person in the play, Mercutio is a kinsman to Prince Escalus (the relation is unspecified). Romeo's good friend, he is the play's champion of sense over romance, self over idealism.

Which is not to say he is without a code—his code springs from the inherited hostility of Verona. And as a young man he brandishes this code proudly, without the tempering influence of adult responsibilities. The near perfect Machiavel, Mercutio's irrepressible appeal to realism permeates his every word.

A PLAGUE
O' BOTH YOUR HOUSES

Mercutio's wit is the source of his strength and he uses it in an attempt to reintegrate the love-estranged Romeo into their circle. He also uses it to defend that circle's honor against Tybalt's challenge (he misreads Romeo's pacifism) and dies when Romeo blocks his vision while trying to end the fighting. With his dying breath, Mercutio curses both households, foreshadowing the tragic deaths of the young lovers.

MERCURIAL
Shakespeare bestowed on Mercutio the volatility inferred by the fleet-footed messenger of the Roman pantheon. Thus, our shorthand symbol for him will be the winged foot of Mercury.

MAB
Mercutio's most famous oration is his Queen Mab speech of 1.4. On the way to the Capulet feast, Mercutio fuses myth and cynicism to parody Romeo's romantic depression and foreboding— ultimately hoping to demonstrate the uselessness of his good friend's moody demeanor.

SWEET FLOWER,

with flowers thy bridal bed I strew—
O woe! Thy canopy is dust and stones—
Which with sweet water nightly I will dew,
Or, wanting that, with tears distill'd by moans;
The obsequies that I for thee will keep
Nightly shall be to strew thy grave and weep.

5.3.12-17

ANSWER
The prince commutes Romeo's sentence to banishment for avenging his kinsman's death.

QUESTION
Where is Mercutio headed when he makes his famous Queen Mab speech? (ANSWER ON PAGE 47)

THIS IS JULIET'S SUITOR

PARIS, LIKE MERCUTIO, IS an unspecified relation to the prince. He is referred to as County Paris, meaning he is a count, equivalent to an earl. His age is never indicated, but for all purposes he embodies the rational maturity absent from Romeo's passionate romanticism.

From 1.2 on, Paris is seen as the persistent suitor of Juliet—or more accurately, the suitor of Capulet, since he lacks either the skill or desire to woo anyone other than her ambitious father. Capulet invites Paris to his feast so the count can win Juliet's affections, but the plan backfires when Romeo famously embraces the task.

WHY, HE'S
A MAN OF WAX

Knowing Romeo only as the killer of his betrothed's cousin, Paris confronts Romeo at the site of Juliet's tomb, attempting to arrest him for violating the terms of his banishment. Romeo tries in vain to scare Paris off, reluctantly fights and kills him, and then—at Paris' dying request—lays him in Juliet's tomb.

COMPLICATION
The terse, rational character of Paris is countervailed at the tomb of Juliet as he is shown genuinely grieving over the death of his promised bride. In a belated display of true emotion, Paris vows to cover her grave daily with tears and flowers, our shorthand symbol for the count.

prince

Escalus
PRINCE OF VERONA

Aloof for much of the play, the prince interrupts the general riot and decrees that the next to disturb his city's peace will pay with their lives. Lady Capulet demands that Romeo be put to death for killing Tybalt, but the prince fairly reduces his sentence to banishment. Prince Escalus is called to the tomb after the bodies are found. After pardoning the friar, he scolds the patriarchs and closes with an admonition to meditate on the events that have transpired.

crown

kinsman   *kinsman*

Mercutio
YOUNG GENTLEMAN

Romeo's friend, Mercutio is the champion of
sense over romance. He wishes to contain
Romeo within the boundaries of his cadre of
adolescent males—of which he is the head—
hallmarked by its violence and cavalier view
of love. Thus, Mercutio is appalled by
Romeo's loving answer to Tybalt's challenge
and he fights Juliet's cousin himself. He is
stabbed when Romeo steps between them.
He dies cursing both houses.

Paris
COUNT

Equivalent to an earl, Paris is Juliet's
persistent suitor, but only in negotiation
with her ambitious father. He is invited
to the Capulet feast to woo Juliet, but
Romeo—better suited to the task—
unknowingly usurps his role. At Juliet's
tomb, Paris confronts Romeo for
violating his banishment and is killed
trying to arrest him. Romeo grants Paris'
dying wish to be buried with Juliet.

winged foot

tear and flower

ANSWER Mercutio is headed with his friends to the Capulet feast when he makes his famous Queen Mab speech.

A QUICK REVIEW *of*

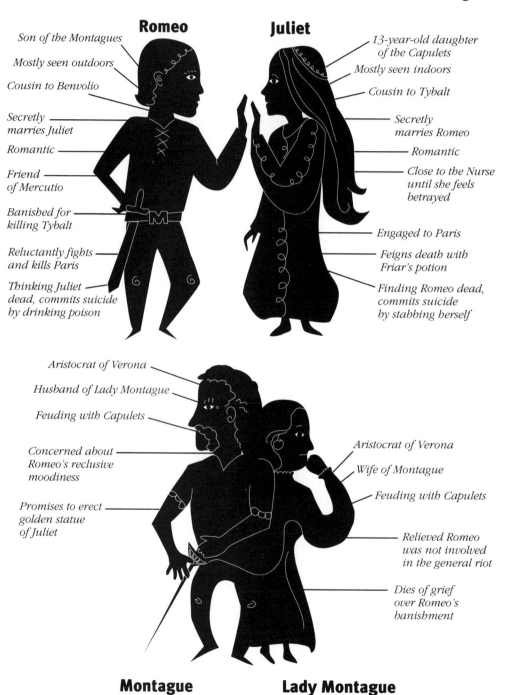

Romeo

Son of the Montagues

Mostly seen outdoors

Cousin to Benvolio

Secretly marries Juliet

Romantic

Friend of Mercutio

Banished for killing Tybalt

Reluctantly fights and kills Paris

Thinking Juliet dead, commits suicide by drinking poison

Juliet

13-year-old daughter of the Capulets

Mostly seen indoors

Cousin to Tybalt

Secretly marries Romeo

Romantic

Close to the Nurse until she feels betrayed

Engaged to Paris

Feigns death with Friar's potion

Finding Romeo dead, commits suicide by stabbing herself

Aristocrat of Verona

Husband of Lady Montague

Feuding with Capulets

Concerned about Romeo's reclusive moodiness

Promises to erect golden statue of Juliet

Aristocrat of Verona

Wife of Montague

Feuding with Capulets

Relieved Romeo was not involved in the general riot

Dies of grief over Romeo's banishment

Montague

Lady Montague

THE MAJOR CHARACTERS

The Nurse

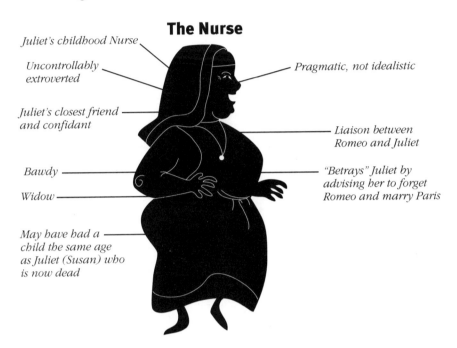

Juliet's childhood Nurse

Uncontrollably extroverted

Juliet's closest friend and confidant

Bawdy

Widow

May have had a child the same age as Juliet (Susan) who is now dead

Pragmatic, not idealistic

Liaison between Romeo and Juliet

"Betrays" Juliet by advising her to forget Romeo and marry Paris

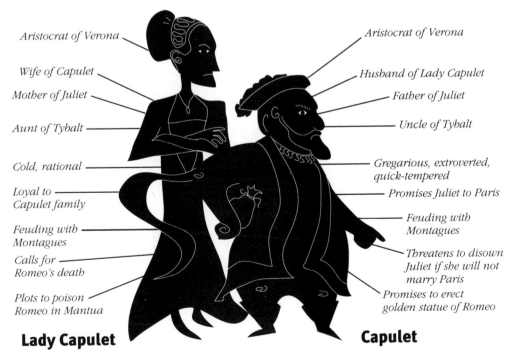

Aristocrat of Verona

Wife of Capulet

Mother of Juliet

Aunt of Tybalt

Cold, rational

Loyal to Capulet family

Feuding with Montagues

Calls for Romeo's death

Plots to poison Romeo in Mantua

Lady Capulet

Aristocrat of Verona

Husband of Lady Capulet

Father of Juliet

Uncle of Tybalt

Gregarious, extroverted, quick-tempered

Promises Juliet to Paris

Feuding with Montagues

Threatens to disown Juliet if she will not marry Paris

Promises to erect golden statue of Romeo

Capulet

A QUICK REVIEW *of*

The Friar

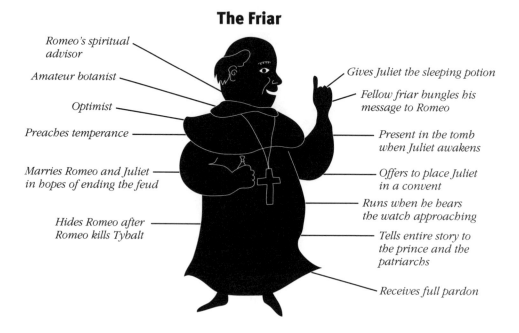

Romeo's spiritual advisor

Amateur botanist

Optimist

Preaches temperance

Marries Romeo and Juliet in hopes of ending the feud

Hides Romeo after Romeo kills Tybalt

Gives Juliet the sleeping potion

Fellow friar bungles his message to Romeo

Present in the tomb when Juliet awakens

Offers to place Juliet in a convent

Runs when he hears the watch approaching

Tells entire story to the prince and the patriarchs

Receives full pardon

Young gentleman of Verona

Cousin to Romeo

Peace loving

Counsels Romeo to attend the Capulet feast

Tells the prince the details of Tybalt's death

Only surviving member of his peer group

Young gentleman of Verona

Cousin to Juliet

Only male Capulet heir

Hot-headed, slow-witted

Offended by Romeo's presence at the feast

Challenges Romeo to a fight

Kills Mercutio when Romeo steps between them

Killed by Romeo

Buried in Capulet family tomb

Benvolio   **Tybalt**

THE MAJOR CHARACTERS

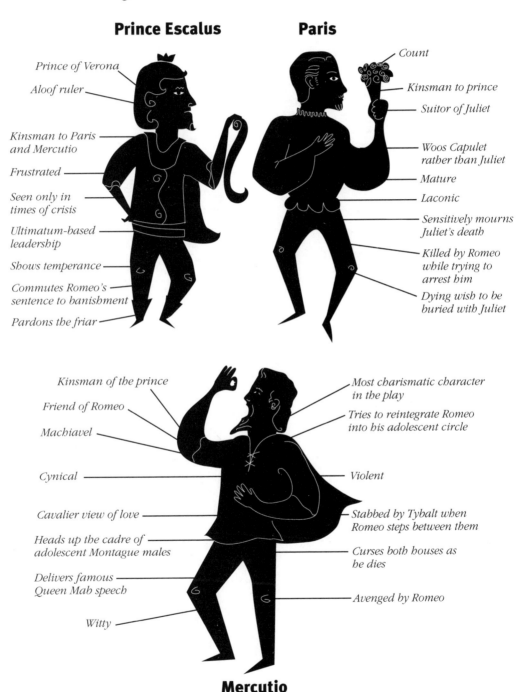

Prince Escalus

- Prince of Verona
- Aloof ruler
- Kinsman to Paris and Mercutio
- Frustrated
- Seen only in times of crisis
- Ultimatum-based leadership
- Shows temperance
- Commutes Romeo's sentence to banishment
- Pardons the friar

Paris

- Count
- Kinsman to prince
- Suitor of Juliet
- Woos Capulet rather than Juliet
- Mature
- Laconic
- Sensitively mourns Juliet's death
- Killed by Romeo while trying to arrest him
- Dying wish to be buried with Juliet

Mercutio

- Kinsman of the prince
- Friend of Romeo
- Machiavel
- Cynical
- Cavalier view of love
- Heads up the cadre of adolescent Montague males
- Delivers famous Queen Mab speech
- Witty
- Most charismatic character in the play
- Tries to reintegrate Romeo into his adolescent circle
- Violent
- Stabbed by Tybalt when Romeo steps between them
- Curses both houses as he dies
- Avenged by Romeo

the Minor *characters*

The minor characters are of much less significance to the plot of Romeo and Juliet *than they are in many of Shakespeare's later tragedies. Peter, the Capulet servants and the clown add a necessary comedic element. The servants help to perpetuate the violence that contaminates every level of Veronese society. Sometimes the minor characters are used as foils: contrasts to underscore the distinctive traits of a major character. Rosaline's rejection of Romeo, for example, heightens the power of Juliet's immediate and complete acceptance; the finality of the apothecary's poison plays counter to the desperate hope of the friar's sleeping potion.*

'TIS WELL THOU ART

*not fish; if thou hadst, thou
hadst been poor John. Draw thy tool! Here comes
two of the house of the Montagues.*

1.1.28-30

QUESTION
How is Paris killed and where is he buried? (ANSWER ON PAGE 56)

THE SERVANTS

SAMPSON, GREGORY
The Capulet servants

After a bit of adolescent wordplay with one another on a Sunday morning in Verona, these two Capulet servants turn their aggression toward their Montague counterparts, Abraham and Balthazar. The resulting quarrel—a comedic parody of the dramatic violence we will see in the main action—shows that the feud has indeed infected all levels of Veronese society. The quarrel erupts into a general riot, stopped only by the intervention of the prince.

ABRAHAM, BALTHAZAR
The Montague servants

The analogues to Sampson and Gregory, these two Montague servants are drawn into the servants' quarrel in the opening scene. Balthazar's role in the play extends beyond that of any servant, with the possible exception of the Nurse's attendant, Peter. Balthazar shuttles messages to Romeo after his banishment, including the information that Juliet has died. He is, of course, fatefully wrong, being fooled like the others by the friar's dubious strategy.

ANTHONY, POTPAN, SERVANTS 1 and 2
Capulet's hired domestic help

Shakespeare uses these servants to create a domestic bustle around the Capulet household. They "cleanse the stage," so to speak, after Mercutio's charismatic Queen Mab speech, making way for Romeo and Juliet's magical first meeting. As the servants bicker, they clear the dishes and prepare the room for the dancing masquers. Their argument adds to the instability of the evening, maintaining the tension caused by a Montague in the Capulet house.

NOW I'LL TELL YOU

*without asking; my master is the
great rich Capulet; and if you be not of the house
of the Montagues, I pray, come and crush a cup of wine.
Rest you merry!*

1.2.80-83

ANSWER

Paris is reluctantly stabbed by Romeo, who lays him in Juliet's tomb, honoring his dying request.

QUESTION

Who begins the quarrel in Act One? (ANSWER ON PAGE 58)

THE SERVANTS

PETER
The Nurse's attendant

Carrying the Nurse's fan, Peter accompanies her on an errand to learn of Romeo's plans for the wedding. Mercutio and Romeo make fun of the Nurse's formal attire. Afterward, she scolds Peter for not defending her. Peter is also seen after Juliet is found "dead," when he tells the musicians hired for the wedding that they will not be paid.

THE PAGES
Tybalt, Mercutio and Paris' attendants

Both Tybalt and Mercutio have anonymous pages— They are asked to fetch a rapier and a surgeon, respectively. Paris' page, however, has a more expanded role. He stands watch a short distance from the tomb as Paris mourns Juliet. After he sees Paris and Romeo fighting, he runs to call the watch. Once the lovers are dead, he is seen leading the watch to the gravesite. He recounts the story to Prince Escalus, telling him of the fight between Paris and Romeo.

THE CLOWN
Sent to invite the guests to the feast

The illiterate clown, a servant of Capulet, is assigned to invite everyone on the guest list to the Capulet feast that evening. Once he is out of sight, however, he admits that he is unable to complete his task without the assistance of a learned gentleman. Romeo and Benvolio happen by and the clown gratefully enlists Romeo's help. Reading the list, Romeo discovers that Rosaline will be attending. The clown shows his thanks by inviting them to the feast, not knowing them to be Montagues.

PUT THIS

in any liquid thing you will,
And drink it off; and, if you had the strength
Of twenty men, it would dispatch you straight.

5.1.81-83

ANSWER
The Capulet servants, Sampson and Gregory, bite their thumb and frown at Abraham and Balthazar.

QUESTION
When Juliet is found "dead," who tells the wedding musicians they won't be paid? (ANSWER ON PAGE 60)

THE FAMILY

CAPULET'S COUSIN
Reminisces with Capulet at the feast

At the feast, Capulet orders the servants to prepare the room for dancing. He turns to his cousin and comments that they are both past their prime. The two then disagree goodheartedly about when they last attended a masque—the wedding of someone named Lucretio—which was at least 25 years previous. Capulet's cousin is not seen again in the play.

ROSALINE—CAPULET'S NIECE
Refuses Romeo's affection

Though never seen in the play, Rosaline is talked of a great deal. She is as much a Capulet as Tybalt, being Capulet's niece. As the play opens, Romeo is lovesick for Rosaline, who will not return his affection. The promise of her attendance at the Capulet feast is his reason for going there with Benvolio. After he meets Juliet, of course, Romeo forgets all about Rosaline—although Mercutio remains under the mistaken belief that Romeo is in love with her.

THE APOTHECARY

IMPOVERISHED DRUGGIST
Sells Romeo poison

After Romeo hears the misguided news of Juliet's death, he remembers an apothecary in Mantua who, because of his poverty, seemed he could be bribed to sell poison (the penalty for which was death). Romeo is correct—although the impoverished druggist resists at first—and eventually obtains the poison for a large amount of money.

THE GROUND IS BLOODY.

Search about the churchyard:
Go, some of you, whoe'er you find attach.
Pitiful sight! Here lies the county slain,
And Juliet bleeding, warm, and newly dead,
Who here hath lain these two days buried...

5.3.181-185

ANSWER
After Juliet is presumed dead, Peter tells the musicians hired to play at her wedding
that they will not be paid.

QUESTION
Romeo buys poison from an apothecary in what city? (ANSWER ON PAGE 62)

THE GUARD

OFFICER
Enlists citizens to beat the quarrelers

With the participation of Benvolio and Tybalt, the servants' quarrel enlarges into a brawl. As it does so, citizens crowd around. An officer rallies the crowd to stop the fighting, yelling to beat both the Montagues and Capulets with clubs and bladed weapons. Of course, his good-intentioned rally cry fuels a full-scale riot as people pour into the fray on all sides. The prince halts the fighting and orders that anyone again disturbing the peace in Verona will be put to death.

WATCHMEN 1, 2 AND 3
Arrive to investigate matters at the tomb

The friar warns Romeo to dodge the watch on his way to Juliet's house the night of his wedding. Later in the play, once Juliet has awakened in the tomb, the friar runs away upon hearing the watch approach. By the time the watch arrive, Juliet has killed herself. The first watchman sends someone to bring the prince, while watchman 2 and 3 apprehend Balthazar and Friar Lawrence.

THE FRANCISCAN

FRIAR JOHN
Bungles the message to Romeo

Friar John was to deliver the letter to Romeo telling of Juliet's feigned death, but returns unsuccessful. He relates that he sought a fellow Franciscan as a travel companion, who he found visiting a house of the sick. Fatefully, both friars were then quarantined to ensure they were not infected with the plague. Alarmed at this news, Friar Lawrence sends Friar John to fetch a crowbar as he plans to be at the tomb before Juliet awakes.

TWO HOUSEHOLDS,

both alike in dignity,
In fair Verona, where we lay our scene,
From ancient grudge break to new mutiny,
Where civil blood makes civil hands unclean.
From forth the fatal loins of these two foes
A pair of star-cross'd lovers take their life...

1.0.1-6

ANSWER
Romeo buys poison from a destitute apothecary in Mantua.

QUESTION
Who do the watchmen apprehend at Juliet's tomb? (ANSWER ON PAGE 65)

THE CHORUS

PROLOGUE TO ACTS ONE AND TWO
Omniscient conscience

The sonnet-speaking chorus introduces Acts One and Two of the play. Before Act One, the chorus raises the themes of longstanding violence and young love—telling us the two will bring about each other's destruction. Before Act Two, the chorus tells us that Romeo and Juliet's love has replaced the dying infatuation Romeo had for Rosaline. The chorus reminds us that Romeo and Juliet's love is as powerful as the forces working against it.

THE CITIZENS

PEOPLE OF VERONA
Riot while beating down the quarrelers

The citizens of Verona join the fight between the Montagues and the Capulets, transforming it into a riot. They bring clubs, hook-bladed bills and double-bladed partisans. Eventually, the prince arrives to stop the fight and make his fateful ruling: anyone disturbing the peace again will be put to death.

THE MUSICIANS

SIMON CATLING, HUGH HREBEC, JAMES SOUNDPOST
Musicians hired for Juliet's wedding

The musicians are packing up their instruments when Peter requests they play a traditional, lively dirge to make him happier. The musicians refuse, thinking it in poor taste. Angry at this, Peter asks them a riddle which no one can correctly answer. The correct answer, which Peter must supply himself, means the musicians will not be paid.

A QUICK REVIEW *of*

The Servants

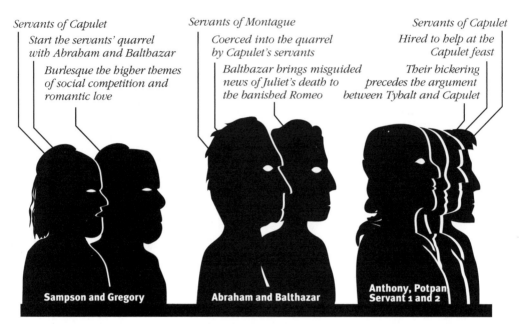

Servants of Capulet
- Start the servants' quarrel with Abraham and Balthazar
- Burlesque the higher themes of social competition and romantic love

Servants of Montague
- Coerced into the quarrel by Capulet's servants
- Balthazar brings misguided news of Juliet's death to the banished Romeo

Servants of Capulet
- Hired to help at the Capulet feast
- Their bickering precedes the argument between Tybalt and Capulet

Sampson and Gregory

Abraham and Balthazar

Anthony, Potpan Servant 1 and 2

The Family

Capulet's niece; never seen
- Romeo is infatuated with her in the beginning of the play
- Mercutio believes Romeo is in love with her the entire play
- Reminisces with Capulet at the feast

The Apothecary

Impoverished druggist in Mantua who sells Romeo the poison he drinks at the tomb

The Guard

Find the bodies in the tomb
- Hold Balthazar and the friar for questioning
- Yells for the citizens to end the servants' quarrel, causing a riot

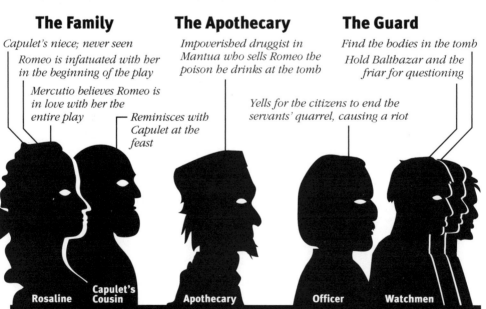

Rosaline **Capulet's Cousin**

Apothecary

Officer **Watchmen**

THE MINOR CHARACTERS

The Servants

The Nurse's attendant

Accompanies her on secret trip to visit Romeo

Tells the musicians they will not be paid

Tybalt's page sent to fetch his rapier at the Capulet feast

Mercutio's page sent to fetch a surgeon

Paris' page accompanies him to Juliet's tomb.

Illiterate

Sent to invite guests to the Capulet feast. Needs Romeo's help.

Invites Romeo to the feast, not knowing him to be a Montague

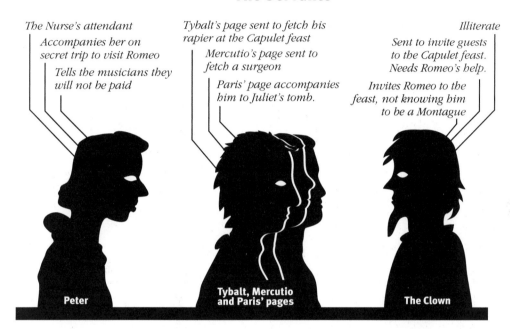

Peter

Tybalt, Mercutio and Paris' pages

The Clown

The Franciscan

Bungles the message to Romeo

Seeks a fellow friar to travel with him to Mantua

Quarantined for suspicion of plague

The Chorus

Impartial commentary; speaks only in sonnet before first two acts.

The Musicians

Hired to play at Juliet's wedding.

Argue with Peter who refuses to pay them

The Citizens

Try to beat down those involved in the servants' quarrel

Escalate the fight into a riot.

Friar John

The Chorus

Simon Catling, Hugh Hrebec, James Soundpost

People of Verona

The
language

The sublime poetry and rhetorical masterwork that forms the foundation of Romeo and Juliet *was a tactical breakthrough for Shakespeare in his career as a playwright. Shakespeare reverse engineered the expansive vocabulary of Petrarchan metaphor, populating his play with animations of their actions, their dialogues and their personifications. The language of* Romeo and Juliet *is its gift, defining the limits of passionate expression. Centuries after, the Pilgrim Sonnet still causes us to swoon; the Queen Mab speech still makes us laugh; the Aubade and the tomb scene still bring us to tears.*

R & J

Romeo and Juliet is a showcase of the English language.

REVOLUTION. With *Romeo and Juliet,* Shakespeare revolutionized the manner in which theatrical drama is written. Though wonderfully extravagant, it cannot be over-emphasized that the rhetoric of *Romeo and Juliet* is not simply flamboyant: it shapes character, moves plot and gives structure to the play. *Romeo and Juliet* is, indeed, the most overt use of language for these purposes of any of Shakespeare's plays.

RHETORIC. Rhetoric is the way language is constructed—the technique of writing. The profusion of rhetoric in *Romeo and Juliet* transcends even the best textbook examples. For instance, Romeo and Juliet speak a love sonnet before their first kiss in 1.5; he and Mercutio competitively trade puns to solidify their adolescent bond in 2.4; Juliet has an outburst of oxymorons (juxtaposed contradictions) in 3.2, to demonstrate her ambivalent frustration with and love for Romeo, who has just been banished. These rhetorical devices and hundreds like them abound in the play, with Shakespeare choosing the appropriate device for the appropriate occasion.

Sonnet metaphors form the foundation of *Romeo and Juliet.*

PETRARCH. Francesco Petrarch lived in 14th century Italy and France. He perfected a poetic form of 14 highly structured lines, now known as the Italian sonnet. In his seminal work *Songs,* Petrarch published 317 sonnets—known as a sequence—exploring his unrequited romantic love for Laura, a woman he met in his early twenties. This work would influence poets for centuries.

METAPHOR. Petrarch's sonnets abound in conceits, which are simply emotional metaphors. Through hundreds of sonnets, Petrarch developed an exhaustive vocabulary of conceits, known as Petrarchan metaphors. Shakespeare laced this well-known vocabulary of Petrarchan metaphors throughout the entire length of his play, anthropomorphizing them with his various characters. In *Romeo and Juliet,* Shakespeare's characters speak in Petrarchan metaphor, act out Petrarchan metaphors and, sometimes, are themselves Petrarchan metaphors (for example, Romeo and Juliet are an animation of the Petrarchan metaphor of the "dear enemy.") *Romeo and Juliet* is thus the dramatic application of the Petrarchan metaphor.

The 14-line sonnet begins here. English sonnets took on the rhyme scheme of four quatrains and a couplet: abab cdcd efef gg.

Here, Romeo touches Juliet's hand, the first step toward his goal of winning a kiss. The "holy shrine" he refers to is Juliet's body.

Makes my flesh tremble in their different greeting.
I will withdraw: but this intrusion shall
Now seeming sweet convert to bitter gall.   *Exit*

ROMEO If I profane with my unworthiest hand   91
This holy shrine, the gentle sin is this:
My lips, two blushing pilgrims, ready stand
To smooth that rough touch with a tender kiss.

Juliet refers to statues of saints that pilgrims touch in devotion.

JULIET Good pilgrim, you do wrong your hand too much,
Which mannerly devotion shows in this;
For saints have hands that pilgrims' hands do touch,
And palm to palm is holy palmers' kiss.

ROMEO Have not saints lips, and holy palmers too?

JULIET Ay, pilgrim, lips that they must use in prayer.

ROMEO O, then, dear saint, let lips do what hands do;
They pray, grant thou, lest faith turn to despair.

Juliet is telling him she'll stand still as a statue if he wants to kiss her.

JULIET Saints do not move, though grant for prayers' sake.

Of course, the effect of Romeo's prayer is to kiss Juliet. The final couplet is punctuated nicely with a kiss.

ROMEO Then move not, while my prayer's effect I take.
Thus from my lips, by yours, my sin is purged.

JULIET Then have my lips the sin that they have took.

ROMEO Sin from thy lips? O trespass sweetly urged!
Give me my sin again.

JULIET You kiss by the book.

NURSE Madam, your mother craves a word with you.

The Pilgrim Sonnet: Romeo and Juliet's first kiss.

FORM. In Shakespeare's day, the sonnet form was a popularly accepted, highly structured means for expressing sexual passion. As such, the sonnet was a contradiction—a rigid, elegantly cordial structure for expressing explosive, unbridled desire. Shakespeare used this poetic form as the medium of exchange for Romeo and Juliet's erotically-charged first meeting; at the Capulet feast they speak alternate lines of a sonnet to one another, punctuating their final couplet with a kiss.

THEME. A pilgrim is a religious devotee who travels to a place of sacred significance. Christians who made pilgrimage to the tomb of Christ were called palmists, being identified with the palm branches Christ's followers greeted him with when he entered Jerusalem. Romeo's name means, "wanderer" or "pilgrim," so Shakespeare chose this definition as the theme of his sonnet: Romeo is a pilgrim come to pay homage at the shrine of Juliet's body, represented as the holy statue of a saint. In the sonnet, note how effortlessly the palmist (branch) conceit gives rise to the palm (hand) metaphor, while the action of touching hands anticipates the action of touching lips.

Juliet begins with an exhortation to speed, directed at the sun god's chariot horses, saying Phaeton—the god's son—would certainly drive faster. Direct address of an absent character, used throughout this soliloquy, is the rhetorical device of apostrophe.

The first erotic reference as "love-performing night" introduces the reason for Juliet's restlessness.

JULIET Gallop apace, you fiery-footed steeds,   1
Towards Phoebus' lodging. such a wagoner
As Phaethon would whip you to the west,
And bring in cloudy night immediately.
Spread thy close curtain, love-performing night,
That runaway's eyes may wink and Romeo
Leap to these arms, untalk'd of and unseen.
Lovers can see to do their amorous rites
By their own beauties; or, if love be blind,
It best agrees with night. Come, civil night,
Thou sober-suited matron, all in black,
And learn me how to lose a winning match,
Play'd for a pair of stainless maidenhoods.
Hood my unmann'd blood, bating in my cheeks,
With thy black mantle; till strange love, grown bold,
Think true love acted simple modesty.
Come, night; come, Romeo; come, thou day in night;
For thou wilt lie upon the wings of night
Whiter than new snow on a raven's back.
Come, gentle night, come, loving, black-brow'd night,
Give me my Romeo; and, when he shall die,
Take him and cut him out in little stars,
And he will make the face of heaven so fine
That all the world will be in love with night
And pay no worship to the garish sun.
O, I have bought the mansion of a love,
But not possess'd it, and, though I am sold,
Not yet enjoy'd: so tedious is this day
As is the night before some festival
To an impatient child that hath new robes
And may not wear them. O, here comes my nurse,

Night is now a woman of experience to teach Juliet to win love by the surrender of her virginity.

Juliet describes herself as an untrained bird who needs a hood to calm her down.

An economic metaphor for Juliet's inexperience: a house paid for but not yet lived in.

Juliet ends by describing herself as an impatient child before a holiday, anxious to wear new clothes for the occasion.

Here "die" doubles as a euphemism for "orgasm."

The Epithalamium: Juliet waits for her bridegroom.

FORM. An epithalamium is an ancient form of lyric poem honoring a bride and her groom. From the Greek meaning, "nuptial" (literally, "at the chamber)," in classical drama an epithalamium was sung by the chorus when the bride was led to her chamber, complete with fabulous mythological creatures sharing in the lover's joy.

THEME. In 3.2, Shakespeare varies the theme with young Juliet waiting anxiously for Romeo's arrival to share their wedding night. She does not yet know that he has killed Tybalt and subsequently been banished. Juliet's metaphors begin with her exhortation for speed directed to the chariot horses of Phoebus, Greek god of the sun. She then anthropomorphizes night as an experienced woman who can teach her how to win love by surrendering her virginity. Playing on the word "maidenhood," her metaphor switches to herself as a hooded falcon—untrained by man—fluttering nervously on her perch. Lastly, Juliet likens herself to an uninhabited house and an impatient child the night before a holiday.

JULIET Wilt thou be gone? it is not yet near day.   1
  It was the nightingale, and not the lark,
  That pierced the fearful hollow of thine ear;
  Nightly she sings on yon pomegranate tree.
  Believe me, love, it was the nightingale.

ROMEO It was the lark, the herald of the morn,
  No nightingale. Look, love, what envious streaks
  Do lace the severing clouds in yonder east:
  Night's candles are burnt out, and jocund day
  Stands tiptoe on the misty mountain tops.
  I must be gone and live, or stay and die.

JULIET Yon light is not daylight, I know it, I.
  It is some meteor that the sun exhales,
  To be to thee this night a torch-bearer,
  And light thee on thy way to Mantua:
  Therefore stay yet; thou need'st not to be gone.

ROMEO Let me be ta'en, let me be put to death;
  I am content, so thou wilt have it so.
  I'll say yon grey is not the morning's eye;
  'Tis but the pale reflex of Cynthia's brow.
  Nor that is not the lark, whose notes do beat
  The vaulty heaven so high above our heads.
  I have more care to stay than will to go.
  Come, death, and welcome! Juliet wills it so.
  How is't, my soul? let's talk; it is not day.

JULIET It is, it is: hie hence, be gone, away!
  It is the lark that sings so out of tune,
  Straining harsh discords and unpleasing sharps.
  Some say the lark makes sweet division;
  This doth not so, for she divideth us.
  Some say the lark and loathed toad change eyes,
  O, now I would they had changed voices too!
  Since arm from arm that voice doth us affray,
  Hunting thee hence with hunt's-up to the day,
  O, now be gone; more light and light it grows.

ROMEO More light and light; more dark and dark our woes!

The Aubade: Romeo and Juliet's poetic farewell.

FORM. An aubade is a song evoking daybreak, originally sung by troubadours—traveling poet-musicians of europe in the middle ages. A familiar motif for an aubade was a watchman's warning to lovers that dawn has arrived. Another motif was the reluctant parting of waking lovers. The converse of an aubade is a serenade, an evening song about lovers coming together.

THEME. Romeo's banishment infuses Shakespeare's aubade with a two-fold energy. First, the lovers believe they will not see each other for a great while and, second, Romeo will be put to death if he does not leave. As dawn breaks, Juliet begins the pretense that it is still night. For her, the nightingale is singing and a meteor lights the sky. Romeo gently corrects her, saying it is the lark and the sun. When Juliet protests, Romeo submits to her fantasy, saying he is content to die if she wills it so. The mention of death jolts Juliet from her illusion and she insists he leave immediately. When Romeo finally descends the balcony, Juliet—in a moment of prescience—remarks that he looks pale, like a dead man at the bottom of a tomb.

ROMEO & JULIET   ACT 1, SCENE 5

MERCUTIO O, then, I see Queen Mab hath been with you.   53
   She is the fairies' midwife, and she comes
   In shape no bigger than an agate stone
   On the forefinger of an alderman,
   Drawn with a team of little atomies
   Over men's noses as they lie asleep;
   Her wagon-spokes made of long spiders' legs,
   The cover of the wings of grasshoppers,
   Her traces of the smallest spider's web,
   The collars of the moonshine's watery beams,
   Her whip of cricket's bone, the lash of film,
   Her wagoner a small grey-coated gnat,
   Not so big as a round little worm
   Prick'd from the lazy finger of a maid;
   Her chariot is an empty hazel-nut
   Made by the joiner squirrel or old grub,
   Time out o' mind the fairies' coachmakers.
   And in this state she gallops night by night
   Through lovers' brains, and then they dream of love;
   O'er courtiers' knees, that dream on courtsies straight,
   O'er lawyers' fingers, who straight dream on fees,
   O'er ladies' lips, who straight on kisses dream,
   Which oft the angry Mab with blisters plagues,
   Because their breaths with sweetmeats tainted are.
   Sometime she gallops o'er a courtier's nose,
   And then dreams he of smelling out a suit;
   And sometime comes she with a tithe-pig's tail
   Tickling a parson's nose as a' lies asleep,
   Then dreams, he of another benefice:
   Sometime she driveth o'er a soldier's neck,
   And then dreams he of cutting foreign throats,
   Of breaches, ambuscadoes, Spanish blades,
   Of healths five-fathom deep; and then anon
   Drums in his ear, at which he starts and wakes,
   And being thus frighted swears a prayer or two
   And sleeps again. This is that very Mab
   That plaits the manes of horses in the night,
   And bakes the elflocks in foul sluttish hairs,
   Which once untangled, much misfortune bodes:
   This is the hag, when maids lie on their backs,
   That presses them and learns them first to bear,
   Making them women of good carriage.
   This is she—

ROMEO Peace, peace, Mercutio, peace!
   Thou talk'st of nothing.

MERCUTIO   True, I talk of dreams,
   Which are the children of an idle brain,

Queen Mab: the clash of pragmatism and romanticism.

FORM. Mercutio's best-known moment comes in the form of an extended oration: the Queen Mab speech. Anaphoric lines—deliberately repeated words at the beginning of successive verses—intensify the speech as it progresses. Moreover, the parallelism in the catalogue of dreamers at the speech's midpoint lends a certain formality, reinforcing the speech as a performance, rather than a dialogue.

THEME. On the way to the Capulet feast, the idealistic Romeo confesses he had a dream that warned him not to attend. Pragmatic Mercutio responds with the construction of the imaginary Queen Mab—a form of parody that Mercutio uses to shock Romeo out of his brooding melancholy. Replete with double entendre, the speech assiduously details the mischievous activities of Mab, the impish bringer of dreams. By satirizing this romantic folklore, Mercutio presents his pragmatic world view as an alternative to Romeo's romantic foreboding. When at last Romeo interrupts Mercutio's ramblings, telling him that he speaks of nothing, Mercutio agrees, saying that is straight to his point—like Romeo, he speaks of dreams.

Romeo killed Tybalt only about an hour after the wedding. Emotional juxtapositions abound in the play: alternations of highs and lows.

The Nurse finally clarifies Juliet's confusion: Tybalt is dead and Romeo is banished. Juliet originally misunderstood the Nurse and thought Romeo was dead.

ROMEO & JULIET   ACT 3, SCENE 2

NURSE Tybalt is gone, and Romeo banished; —————— 69
Romeo that killed him, he is banished.

JULIET O God! did Romeo's hand shed Tybalt's blood?

NURSE It did, it did; alas the day, it did!

Juliet begins her outburst of oxymora, revealing her ambivalence— she loves Romeo, but hates that he has jeopardized their hours-old relationship.

JULIET O serpent heart, hid with a flowering face! ——————
Did ever dragon keep so fair a cave?
Beautiful tyrant, fiend angelical,
Dove-feathered raven, wolvish-ravening lamb,
Despised substance of divinest show!
Just opposite to what thou justly seem'st,
A damned saint, an honourable villain!
O nature, what hadst thou to do in hell,
When thou didst bower the spirit of a fiend
In mortal paradise of such sweet flesh?
Was ever book containing such vile matter
So fairly bound? O that deceit should dwell
In such a gorgeous palace!

NURSE There's no trust,
No faith, no honesty in men; all perjured,
All forsworn, all naught, all dissemblers.
Ah, where's my man? Give me some aqua-vitae.
These griefs, these woes, these sorrows make me old.
Shame come to Romeo!

The Nurse's commiseration brings about another emotional switch—Juliet now repents her tirade.

JULIET   Blistered by thy tongue
For such a wish! He was not born to shame.
Upon his brow shame is ashamed to sit;
For 'tis a throne where honour may be crowned
Sole monarch of the universal earth.
O, what a beast was I to chide him!

NURSE Will you speak well of him that killed your cousin?

JULIET Shall I speak ill of him that is my husband?

The biblical vocabulary of serpent, dragon, angel, fiend, ravening wolf, divine, spirit and paradise collectively suggest an image of Satan from Genesis.

The oxymoron: embodiment of love in death.

FORM. Romeo and Juliet are trapped within a dichotomy: they feel compelled to demonstrate their love through death. Therefore, Shakespeare uses the rhetorical device of oxymoron—the juxtaposition of incongruous words—through the entire play. For example, in the servants' quarrel, Tybalt describes Benvolio oxymoronically, "What, drawn and talk of peace?" As the prince breaks up the riot, he calls the citizens "rebellious subjects." Later, Romeo histrionically describes his unrequited love for Rosaline with a string of oxymora, including "brawling love", "loving hate," "heavy lightness," "serious vanity," "feather of lead," "bright smoke," "cold fire" and "sick health." Throughout the play, these rhetorical contradictions reflect the essential dichotomy of dying for love.

THEME. In one of the best known examples of oxymora in the play, Juliet displays her ambivalent feelings upon hearing the news of Romeo's banishment. She describes Romeo with a flood of contradictions, before calming down and repenting of her outburst.

Capulet forms an epitaph for his child that naturally migrates into an epitaph for himself.

Death was a commonly personified concept in the middle ages, typically seen in the morality plays.

ROMEO & JULIET   ACT 4, SCENE 5

FRIAR LAURENCE Come, is the bride ready to go to church?

CAPULET Ready to go, but never to return.   36
  O son, the night before thy wedding-day
  Hath Death lain with thy wife. There she lies,
  Flower as she was, deflowered by him.
  Death is my son-in-law, Death is my heir;
  My daughter he hath wedded: I will die,
  And leave him all; life, living, all is Death's.

PARIS Have I thought long to see this morning's face,
  And doth it give me such a sight as this?

LADY CAPULET Accursed, unhappy, wretched, hateful day!

The metaphoric noun, "flower," doubles as the connotatively destructive verb.

ROMEO & JULIET   ACT 5, SCENE 3

ROMEO Forgive me cousin. Ah, dear Juliet,   101
  Why art thou yet so fair? Shall I believe
  That unsubstantial death is amorous,
  And that the lean abhorred monster keeps
  Thee here in dark to be his paramour?
  For fear of that I still will stay with thee,
  And never from this pallet of dim night
  Depart again. Here, here will I remain
  With worms that are thy chambermaids. O, here
  Will I set up my everlasting rest,
  And shake the yoke of inauspicious stars
  From this world-wearied flesh. Eyes look your last.

Capulet's image of a one time deflowering is replaced by Romeo's image of Juliet's fate as a continual mistress.

This image generates a protective justification for Romeo's suicide: that is, he will keep Juliet from harm.

Romeo and Juliet: a consummation in death.

THRESHOLD. *Romeo and Juliet* ends with the triumph of love over hatred: the families reconcile and Romeo and Juliet's love is immortalized at its zenith, represented by the solid gold statues. The ironic triumph, however, cannot occur without passage through the ultimate terror of violence—namely, death. It is this threshold that must be courageously breached by the lovers before the reconciliation and immortalization can ensue. Romeo is the first to intimate that he is unmoved by the ultimate threat of violence when he says in 3.5, "Come death and welcome. Juliet wills it so."

BRIDE. Juliet is spoken of as death's bride and death's mistress by her father in 4.5 and by Romeo in 5.3, respectively. During these moments Juliet is still in the suspension of sleep brought on by the potion; these moments serve only to foreshadow her genuine death after she awakens. However, even then—when facing the instant of her suicide—Juliet's death takes on a symbolism of sexual consummation as she raises the knife and declares, "O happy dagger, / This is thy sheath."

Plot
overview

The powerful force of Romeo and Juliet
*lies in the war between a young love
refusing to compromise and a punishing,
ancient hatred. The outcome is the
emotionally compelling fulfillment and
extinction and immortalizing of their
love—the conceptual protagonist of the
play. The tragedy begins as a comedy,
complete with Shakespearean clowns, a
cotillion, dancing and love poetry. Then,
with the death of the witty, extroverted
Mercutio, the comedy takes a turn and
becomes a tragedy of pathos,
with innocent victims, bungled
messages, desperate strategies
and a gathering set of
inexorable consequences.*

Romeo and Juliet begins with ancient hatred.

ORIGINLESS. The reason the Montagues and Capulets are feuding is moot—they have been engaged in a seemingly originless, mechanical hatred for generations. Give the feud a motive, no matter how farfetched, and it can be solved with diplomacy. This was intended by Shakespeare: there exists no original trespass because their can be no possible solution. By refusing to delineate a boundary to the feud, Shakespeare enables it to substitute for all hatred. In this sense, the feud becomes the antagonist in the play.

EVERPRESENT. Hatred infuses every pore of the play. It permeates all strata of Veronese life, from servants to aristocrats. It shows itself in many forms: the rape and murder fantasies of Sampson; the duel lust of Tybalt; the violent cynicism of Mercutio; the social ambition of Capulet; the chauvinism of his wife; and the constant bickering of their hired help. Against this juggernaut of violence, the love of Romeo and Juliet will strive.

Let's plot the major instances of violence on a timeline.

We'll lay it out on a line, with regular divisions for each scene. This will help give you a big-picture view of the main plot.

Each of the divisions on the timeline corresponds to one scene of the play. For example, the first division represents Act 1, Scene 1. Don't worry about memorizing in which act or scene an event occurs. Just think about it in terms of the beginning, middle and end of the play.

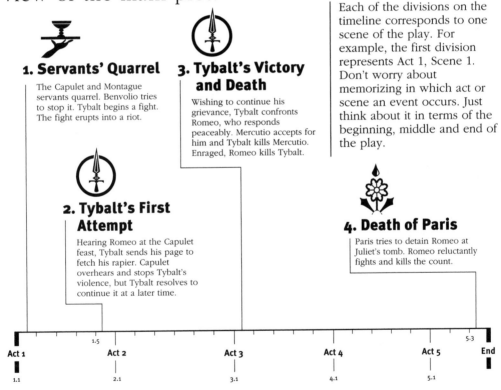

1. Servants' Quarrel

The Capulet and Montague servants quarrel. Benvolio tries to stop it. Tybalt begins a fight. The fight erupts into a riot.

3. Tybalt's Victory and Death

Wishing to continue his grievance, Tybalt confronts Romeo, who responds peaceably. Mercutio accepts for him and Tybalt kills Mercutio. Enraged, Romeo kills Tybalt.

2. Tybalt's First Attempt

Hearing Romeo at the Capulet feast, Tybalt sends his page to fetch his rapier. Capulet overhears and stops Tybalt's violence, but Tybalt resolves to continue it at a later time.

4. Death of Paris

Paris tries to detain Romeo at Juliet's tomb. Romeo reluctantly fights and kills the count.

1.5

Act 1   Act 2   Act 3   Act 4   Act 5   End

5.3

1.1   2.1   3.1   4.1   5.1

Within this world of ageless violence blooms young love.

SUSPENSION. Juliet is not quite fourteen years old. Romeo is a young man. Both hover in the unresolved psychological space between puberty and maturity. It is a liminal space of parenthesis and, as we shall see, their love will attempt to force a similar parenthesis within the all-pervasive violence. Sublime moments rise where the frantic timeframe of the play slows to a crawl and no violence can penetrate. The only meaning is reckoned in Romeo and Juliet's uncompromising love for one another. In this way, their love is the conceptual protagonist of the play.

INTEGRATION. Neither Romeo, nor Juliet desire to remain suspended between the worlds of childhood and adulthood: both wish to cross the threshold of maturity. Their mediator for this task is the friar. It is he who marries them; it is he who sends Romeo to his wedding bed, then on to Mantua with the hope that the families will reconcile and precipitate his return; it is he who devises the final strategy of the sleeping potion. Despite his best attempts to integrate Romeo and Juliet's love into adulthood, the violence that dominates adult life in Verona—against all our best hopes—ultimately rejects it.

Here are the major moments of love on the timeline.

The moments of love in the play press their way between the layers of constant violence in Verona. In these recesses, the lovers create a space for passionate expression—their magical first meeting, promises to marry, clandestine wedding and heartfelt departure. Here is the timeline of those moments:

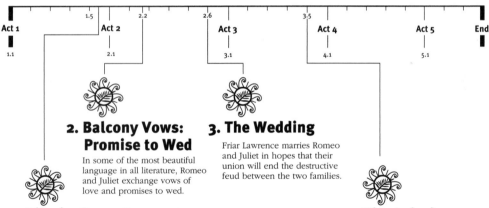

2. Balcony Vows: Promise to Wed

In some of the most beautiful language in all literature, Romeo and Juliet exchange vows of love and promises to wed.

3. The Wedding

Friar Lawrence marries Romeo and Juliet in hopes that their union will end the destructive feud between the two families.

1. Pilgrim Sonnet: The First Kiss

At the Capulet feast, Romeo and Juliet meet for the first time. They speak a sonnet wherein Romeo is a reverent traveler come to pay homage to Juliet, the object of his sacred pilgrimage .

4. The Aubade: Heartfelt Departure

The day after their wedding, in desperately loving language, Juliet pretends it is not yet morning, hoping to delay Romeo's inexorable departure to Mantua.

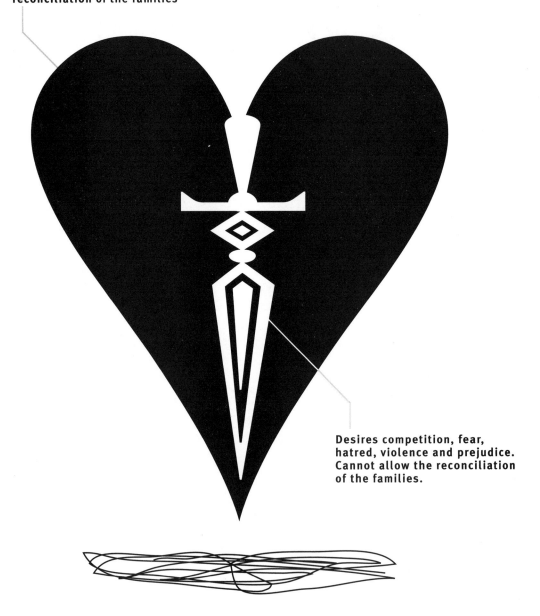

Desires love, passion, romance and harmony. Believes in the reconciliation of the families

Desires competition, fear, hatred, violence and prejudice. Cannot allow the reconciliation of the families.

Violence and love attempt to extinguish each other.

DYSTOPIA. The mindless feud between the Montagues and the Capulets thrives in the hostile adult world of Verona. It is an oppressive dystopia of violence and the competing families nourish their children on its hatred. Capulet stops Tybalt from fighting only because he was scolded that day in a private meeting with the prince. Even the servants reflexively mirror their masters' hostility. This originless, irrational hatred creates an environment with meager hope for love between a Montague and a Capulet—every social transaction increases love's futility and threatens its extinction.

IDYLL. This dystopia is itself threatened by the romantic love between Rome and Juliet. In a renunciation of all that has come before, their love overthrows the status quo and, by sheer force of ideal, refuses to let violence or prejudice or social construct admission through its gates. The stolen moments of love exist in an idyllic dimension all their own, full of passion and optimism and tender dreams of familial reconciliation. It is this youthful drive for restorative love that collides with the ancient, alienating violence that surrounds it—the conflict between the protagonist and antagonist.

Desires love, passion, romance and harmony. Believes in the reconciliation of the families

Desires competition, fear, hatred, violence and prejudice. Cannot allow the reconciliation of the families.

Here is a plot of the violence and love.

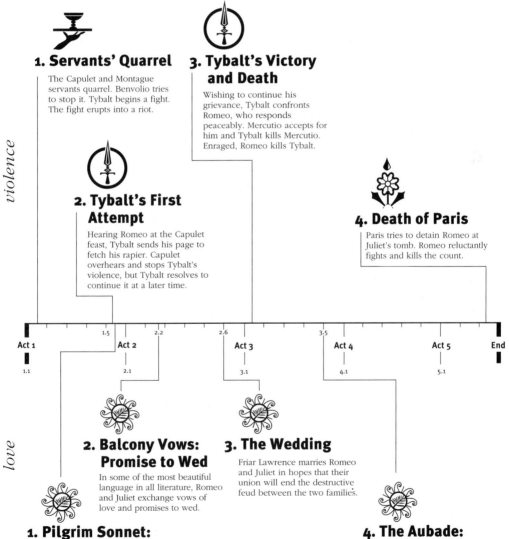

violence

1. Servants' Quarrel

The Capulet and Montague servants quarrel. Benvolio tries to stop it. Tybalt begins a fight. The fight erupts into a riot.

3. Tybalt's Victory and Death

Wishing to continue his grievance, Tybalt confronts Romeo, who responds peaceably. Mercutio accepts for him and Tybalt kills Mercutio. Enraged, Romeo kills Tybalt.

2. Tybalt's First Attempt

Hearing Romeo at the Capulet feast, Tybalt sends his page to fetch his rapier. Capulet overhears and stops Tybalt's violence, but Tybalt resolves to continue it at a later time.

4. Death of Paris

Paris tries to detain Romeo at Juliet's tomb. Romeo reluctantly fights and kills the count.

1.5		2.2		2.6		3.5			
Act 1		Act 2		Act 3		Act 4		Act 5	End
1.1		2.1		3.1		4.1		5.1	

love

2. Balcony Vows: Promise to Wed

In some of the most beautiful language in all literature, Romeo and Juliet exchange vows of love and promises to wed.

3. The Wedding

Friar Lawrence marries Romeo and Juliet in hopes that their union will end the destructive feud between the two families.

1. Pilgrim Sonnet: The First Kiss

At the Capulet feast, Romeo and Juliet meet for the first time. They speak a sonnet wherein Romeo is a reverent traveler come to pay homage to Juliet, the object of his sacred pilgrimage .

4. The Aubade: Heartfelt Departure

The day after their wedding, in desperately loving language, Juliet pretends it is not yet morning, hoping to delay Romeo's inexorable departure to Mantua.

Montague vows to erect a solid gold statue of Juliet in Verona; Capulet reciprocates with one of Romeo. The statues immortalize the victory of Romeo and Juliet's love over the feud.

Love triumphs over violence in an unexpected way.

SUICIDE. When Romeo is misinformed about Juliet's death (she is actually sleeping), he kills himself by drinking poison, choosing to join his love in death rather than be apart from her in life. When she wakes, Juliet follows suit, stabbing herself with Romeo's dagger before the watchmen arrive. How is this double suicide the triumph of love? In two ways: their deaths reconcile the families and freeze their love at the height of its intensity.

RECONCILIATION. The deaths of Romeo and Juliet extinguish the hostility between the Montagues and the Capulets. Upon seeing the bodies of their dead children, the patriarchs shake hands and end their longstanding feud. As the violence once rippled through all social strata, we expect the reconciliation will do so as well.

IMMORTALITY. With their deaths, the adolescent passions of Romeo and Juliet are frozen at their zenith. The emotions cannot now diminish over time or die away. Willing to die for their love, the two claim victory over violence, ironically by doing violence to themselves. They show themselves unafraid of hatred's ultimate terror—death—as it is only death that can reunite them.

Four days in Verona: A chronology of love's triumph.

Day One: Sunday

Servants' riot; Capulet feast; first kiss

On a mid-July morning, the Montague and Capulet servants quarrel. Benvolio tries to stop it and Tybalt confronts him—a riot ensues. The prince rules that anyone disturbing the peace again will be put to death. He demands to speak privately with each patriarch.

Romeo enters and Benvolio advises his lovesick cousin to forget Rosaline and find another girl. That afternoon, Capulet hears Paris' request to marry Juliet and invites him to a feast for the purpose of wooing her. The clown is sent to invite guests to the feast and Romeo—helping the illiterate servant to read the guest list—discovers Rosaline will be there. The clown, not knowing Romeo is a Montague, invites him to the feast as thanks for his assistance. Early that evening, Lady Capulet tells Juliet of Paris' intentions with the Nurse present. The Nurse is ecstatic. Juliet says she will do as her mother advises her.

That night, Romeo, Benvolio and Mercutio walk to the Capulet feast. On the way, Mercutio tries to dissuade Romeo from his brooding melancholy. Once at the feast, Romeo meets Juliet and they share their first magical kiss. Incensed at seeing a Montague, Tybalt tells his page to fetch his rapier. Capulet overhears his nephew and scolds him for disturbing the celebration. He reminds Tybalt that only hours before he was reprimanded by the prince in a private meeting. Tybalt relents, resolving to continue his grievance another time. After the feast, Romeo hides in Capulet's garden and waits for Mercutio and Benvolio to go home. He returns to find Juliet on her balcony, bemoaning her fateful love of a Montague—de facto enemy of her family. They exchange vows of love and promises to marry.

Four days in Verona: A chronology of love's triumph.

Day Two: Monday

Wedding; two deaths, banishment; the arranged marriage

Romeo, after staying up all night, finds Friar Lawrence gathering herbs. After some resistance, he convinces the friar to perform his wedding to Juliet. The friar is hopeful the marriage will end the bitter feud.

At noon, the Nurse finds Romeo. He tells the Nurse to have Juliet meet him at Friar Lawrence's in a few hours, under the pretense of confession, where they can be married. He pays the Nurse, who then takes word to Juliet. Juliet is overjoyed at the news. She meets Romeo at the friar's and the two are wed.

A short hour later, Tybalt searches for Romeo to challenge him for his trespass at the Capulet feast. He approaches Mercutio and Benvolio, asking if they know the whereabouts of Romeo, but Mercutio interrupts him with insulting wit. Romeo enters and Tybalt challenges him to a fight. Romeo declines, answering peaceably and lovingly since Tybalt is his new wife's cousin. Mercutio, misreading Romeo's reply, fights Tybalt in Romeo's stead. Romeo steps between them and Tybalt stabs Mercutio beneath Romeo's arm, killing him. Enraged, Romeo fights and kills Tybalt, then flees before the prince arrives. Lady Capulet calls for the death of Romeo, but the prince fairly commutes his sentence to banishment.

Juliet, waiting for night to fall so that she can be with her new husband, hears news from the Nurse that Romeo has been banished for killing Tybalt. Juliet gives the Nurse a ring to take to Romeo, which she does, finding him weeping at Friar Lawrence's. As night falls, the friar sends Romeo to Juliet, telling him to leave for Mantua before dawn. There he is to await word that the friar has had opportunity to tell the parents of the marriage, thereby reconciling the families.

As Romeo and Juliet secretly celebrate their wedding night in her room, Capulet arranges for Paris to marry Juliet on Thursday.

Four days in Verona: A chronology of love's triumph.

Day Three: Tuesday

Farewell; Juliet's resistance; feigned confession; sleeping potion

As dawn arrives, Romeo and Juliet exchange heartfelt farewells before Romeo leaves for Mantua. Moments later, Lady Capulet informs Juliet of her father's arrangements for her to marry Paris. Juliet protests. Capulet enters and is first confused, then enraged, at Juliet's resistance. He threatens to disown her if she will not marry Paris on Thursday.

After he leaves, Juliet begs her mother to intervene, but she refuses and follows her husband. Desperate, Juliet asks for the Nurse's advice. The Nurse tells her to forget Romeo, who has been banished, and marry Paris, who she believes is a far better man. Juliet's love for the Nurse turns cold and she goes to Friar Lawrence's, once again under the pretense of confession.

At the friar's, Juliet unexpectedly encounters Paris, who is making arrangements for the friar to perform the wedding. She resists his clumsy attempts at intimacy. Once Paris leaves, Juliet tells Friar Lawrence she will kill herself rather than betray Romeo. The friar gives her a sleeping potion instead, telling her it will imitate death. The friar says he will alert Romeo of their plan, who will be there as she awakens to escort her to Mantua.

After she arrives home, Juliet tells her father she has repented her sin of disobedience. Exuberant, Capulet moves the wedding day up to Wednesday, the following morning. That night, in her bedroom, Juliet debates the dangers of the friar's dubious strategy. She hallucinates, seeing Tybalt's ghost searching for Romeo. Calling for him to stop, she toasts her love and drinks the potion.

Four days in Verona: A chronology of love's triumph.

Day Four: Wednesday

Juliet found; the bungled letter; Romeo and Juliet's deaths; reconciliation

Early in the morning, the Capulet household busies itself with the wedding preparations. As Paris arrives, Capulet sends the Nurse to wake Juliet, who finds her and presumes her dead. The house falls into mourning and the friar arrives, counseling the family that Juliet is now in a better place.

Balthazar rides to tell Romeo the misguided news of her death. Distraught, Romeo buys poison in Mantua. That evening, Friar Lawrence discovers that his letter to Romeo was never delivered, because his messenger, Friar John, was quarantined after visiting a house of the sick.

At the tomb, Paris directs his page to signal if anyone approaches. He then scatters flowers before the doorway. The page signals as Romeo and Balthazar approach. Paris quickly hides. Romeo sends Balthazar away and opens the tomb. Paris attempts to arrest him for violating his banishment. After trying to scare Paris off, Romeo reluctantly fights and kills Paris—placing him in the tomb at his dying request. Romeo sees Juliet and remarks at how beautiful she looks in death. He makes a toast to their love, drinks the poison and dies.

The friar enters the tomb as Juliet awakens. He tells her misfortune has altered his plan. Hearing the watchmen approach, he says they must leave and he offers to hide her in a convent. The friar flees, but—seeing her dead Romeo—Juliet takes his dagger and kills herself.

Paris' page leads the watchmen to the tomb. They find the bodies and send for the prince and the patriarchs. Balthazar and the friar are detained for questioning. The prince, Capulet and Montague arrive. Montague says his wife has died of grief. The friar tells the entire tragedy and is pardoned. Capulet reconciles with Montague and the patriarchs agree to end the feud. To memorialize their peace, they resolve to erect golden statues of each other's child in Verona.

Scene
by scene

This chapter serves as a summary of the action and dialogue in each scene of the play. The scene breaks in Shakespeare's plays are arbitrary—they were not noted in the original documents—but, except in rare instances, they occur when the stage completely clears. Romeo and Juliet contains many short scenes (especially in Act Four). These, therefore, have been combined onto a single summary page, as with 4.2 and 4.3. We reccommend you read this chapter in one or two sittings, if time allows, thereby gaining a large, sweeping view of Romeo and Juliet, *before tackling the actual text of the play.*

ACT 1, SCENE 1

The servants riot; the prince's edict; Benvolio's advice to lovesick Romeo.

SAMPSON AND GREGORY, two servants of the Capulet household, talk outdoors on a Sunday morning in Verona. Sampson brags of the violence he would inflict upon anyone he sees from the Montague household—longtime enemy of the Capulets. Gregory, in jest, takes all of Sampson's words literally, which often results in a complete turnaround of their meaning. Frustrated at this, Sampson grows so agitated that he talks of raping the Montague women in the street.

Just then, Gregory points out two Montague servants, Abraham and Balthazar, heading their way. Sampson bites his thumb insultingly as the two Montagues pass. When confronted by Abraham, however, Sampson denies the gesture was intended toward anyone in particular. The resulting quarrel quickly erupts into a swordfight, with Sampson being the first to draw. As the fighting begins, the noble Benvolio, Montague's nephew, appears. He scolds the servants and urges them to put away their weapons. Tybalt, nephew of Lady Capulet, enters and threatens Benvolio.

Benvolio says he is only trying to stop the fight and tries to convince Tybalt, a fellow nobleman, to help him. Tybalt will have nothing of it and instead attacks Benvolio. Several citizens join the fray, and a riot ensues. The aged patriarchs of both families rush to square off in battle, but are prevented by their concerned wives.

The Prince of Verona arrives with his attendants and orders all to throw down their swords. He blames the patriarchs for disturbing the peace three times in the past as a result of their longstanding feud. He orders that anyone disturbing the peace in the future will be put to death. He calls Capulet to come with him and commands Montague to see him later that afternoon.

Everyone leaves except Benvolio, Montague and Lady Montague. Benvolio relates the details of his encounter with Tybalt. Lady Montague expresses relief that her son, Romeo, was not involved in the fighting. Benvolio says that earlier in the morning he saw Romeo hurrying away to be alone. At this, Montague confirms that his son has been puzzlingly introverted, secretive and depressed.

Romeo enters and his parents leave so Benvolio may discover the reason for their son's moodiness. Benvolio speaks with his cousin and learns that he is lovesick over a girl who has sworn a vow of chastity. Benvolio counsels Romeo to forget about this girl and look around at all the other beautiful women in Verona.

CARICATURE
The major themes of romantic love and social competition are distorted in Sampson's rodomontade of rape and murder. This grotesque backdrop of violence helps to accentuate the sublime beauty of Romeo and Juliet's uncompromising love.

ACT 1, SCENE 2

Paris discusses his request to marry Juliet; the Capulet party invitation.

CAPULET AND COUNTY PARIS are mid-conversation. Capulet speaks optimistically about the possibility of peace between his house and the house of Montague. Paris replies politely and then quickly changes the subject to his request for Juliet's hand in marriage. Capulet responds, saying his daughter is too young and naive, being not even fourteen years old. He suggests they wait two more years and then reappraise her readiness for marriage.

Paris points out that girls younger than Juliet are already happy mothers. Capulet concedes the point, but remains firm that marriage at this young age is not an ideal situation. He goes on to say that Juliet is his only remaining child (suggesting he had other children who are now dead). He urges Paris to use the next two years as an opportunity to woo Juliet, thereby securing her affections. Capulet states that his consent to the marriage is less important than Juliet's feelings, but he goes on to say that he will gladly approve the union if Juliet agrees.

Toward this end, Capulet invites County Paris to a traditional feast he is holding that evening where there will be many guests. He says that Paris should plan to see many beautiful women at the feast and then decide if Juliet is still his first choice for marriage.

Capulet hands a guest list for the feast to his servant (who functions as a Shakespearean clown in this play). He tells the servant to find everyone on the list and inform them they are welcome to a feast at the house of Capulet. Capulet and Paris exit, leaving the servant to his task.

The servant, in soliloquy, admits that he is illiterate and cannot fulfill his duty. He concludes that he must find a learned gentleman to assist him. Fortuitously, Romeo and Benvolio enter discussing Romeo's tiresome lovesickness. Benvolio recommends that Romeo seek out another love to get over his rejection. Romeo continues to lament.

The servant asks Romeo if he will read the invitation for him. Romeo complies, discovering Mercutio, Rosaline (who we learn is Romeo's infatuation) and Tybalt among the guests listed. The servant thanks Romeo by inviting him to the feast, not knowing he is a Montague. After the servant exits, Benvolio advises Romeo to go to the feast and see for himself that Rosaline is not the most beautiful. Romeo agrees, not for Benvolio's reason, but to rejoice in the splendor of Rosaline's beauty.

REVERSAL
At this point in the play, Capulet puts his daughter's feelings ahead of his own patriarchal consent. By 3.5, however, he will undergo a complete reversal, threatening Juliet with disownment when she finally makes her feelings known.

ACT 1, SCENE 3

Lady Capulet tells Juliet of Paris' intentions; the Nurse reminisces.

LADY CAPULET TELLS the Nurse to call Juliet. The Nurse complies with a wordy commotion that will define her character. Juliet enters and Lady Capulet dismisses the Nurse for privacy, then calls her back, remembering the Nurse's close relationship with Juliet. Lady Capulet and the Nurse discuss Juliet's blossoming maturity. The Nurse reminds Lady Capulet that Juliet and Susan—a girl, now dead, who was either Juliet's twin or the Nurse's own child—were the same age.

The Nurse says that eleven years have passed since the day Juliet was weaned. She remembers it clearly because there was an earthquake the same day. At that time, she recalls, Capulet and Lady Capulet were traveling in Mantua. Reminiscing further, the Nurse tells a long-winded story in which Juliet fell forward and hurt her head the day before the earthquake. Her fall prompted the Nurse's late husband to pick up the toddler and make a bawdy joke about her falling backward when she grew wiser. The Nurse laughs uncontrollably that the little toddler, Juliet, had actually agreed with him.

Lady Capulet bids the Nurse to hold her peace, but it takes Juliet to halt the Nurse's chortles. Some directors choose to have Lady Capulet join in the Nurse's laughter.

Lady Capulet then asks Juliet directly what her feelings are regarding marriage. Juliet replies respectfully that marriage is honorable, but it is something she has not considered. Her mother says that she should begin to think about it, since Paris has made formal request for her hand.

The Nurse is exuberant at the news; both she and Lady Capulet praise Paris as the most handsome and virtuous man in all Verona. Lady Capulet likens Paris to a beautiful manuscript, waiting for a wonderful, gold-laid cover (Juliet) to share the beauty of his story. Lady Capulet says Juliet's own beauty will be the perfect complement to that of her handsome suitor's. The Nurse finishes Lady Capulet's metaphor with a low-comic, bawdy pun. Lady Capulet asks Juliet to speak her mind plainly as to whether or not she is open to Paris' advances. Juliet replies that she is, but only so far as her mother gives her permission. Juliet's open reception to Paris' suit for marriage (as well as her parents' mediation) will change the moment she meets Romeo.

A servant enters, telling them supper is served and the guests are calling for them. They go to the feast as Lady Capulet tells Juliet that Paris waits to see her.

STEREOTYPE
Juliet's Nurse is a modified medieval stereotype—a bawdy, sexually enthusiastic old woman who facilitates the elicit encounters of young lovers. This stereotype would have been well-recognized by Elizabethan audiences.

ACT 1, SCENE 4

Romeo and his friends go to the Capulet feast; Mercutio's speech.

WEARING MASKS, ROMEO, Mercutio and Benvolio, along with several others walk to the Capulet feast. Romeo is concerned that they will need an introductory speech. Benvolio assures him that such speeches are out of fashion. He tells Romeo not to worry about how they will be received—they will only dance a little and then leave. Romeo asks to carry a torch (a servile role), because his spirits are too heavy to dance. Mercutio speaks up, insisting that Romeo *must* dance.

Using marvelous wordplay, Romeo and Mercutio have a friendly disagreement about the characteristics of love. Mercutio maintains love should elevate lovers and make them lighthearted; Romeo holds the opposite view, saying love is weighing him down and causing him heartache. Mercutio replies that if love is painful, then Romeo should fight back with equal violence, beating love at its own game. He then calls for a mask, saying it will cover his ugliness. The group arrives at the Capulet house. Benvolio tells them to simply enter and begin dancing as soon as they are inside.

Unmoved by his friends, Romeo still declines to dance, saying he will just watch the others. Mercutio urges him to join in. Romeo says it isn't wise for Montagues to be at the Capulet household, since he had a premonition in a dream last night.

Mercutio interrupts, saying obviously the fairy Queen Mab—the fairy of dreams—visited Romeo in his sleep. He launches into a poetic description of Mab: a gemstone-sized fairy with a hazelnut chariot drawn by tiny creatures and driven by a gnat. He says she rides her chariot over sleepers, bringing them appropriate dreams: to lovers she brings dreams of love; to courtiers she brings dreams of courtly life and the promise of suits; to lawyers she brings dreams of payment; to ladies who dream of kisses she brings blisters; to parsons she brings dreams of additional churches; to soldiers she brings dreams of battle. She twists horse's manes and old women's hair at night. She is a type of incubus, pressing on women and teaching them to give birth.

Romeo interrupts when Mercutio's speech reaches a fever pitch. He tells Mercutio that he is speaking nonsense. Mercutio agrees, saying that he speaks of dreams, which are themselves foolish. Benvolio urges them on, warning supper is over and they'll be late. Romeo voices a premonition that something at this party will end his life, but he puts his faith in God and goes in.

DREAMS
Likely of Celtic origin, Queen Mab (meaning "slut") is used by Mercutio to point out the frivolousness of dreams to Romeo. The Queen Mab speech astutely develops the character of Mercutio as an unsentimental pragmatist, setting him counter to Romeo's romantic idealism.

ACT 1, SCENE 5

The feast; Tybalt's anger at Romeo's presence; the Pilgrim Sonnet.

INSIDE THE CAPULET house, as two servants clear the dishes, they complain about the lack of help from another servant, called Potpan. The second servant exits as another servant, Antony, enters with Potpan. Potpan is cheerful and suggests the other servants cheer up as well. Meanwhile, Capulet welcomes Romeo and his friends with assurances that the ladies will dance with them. He directs the musicians to play and the guests to dance, then sits down to reminisce with his cousin.

Romeo notices Juliet and is spellbound. He asks a nearby servant who she is. The servant, perhaps hired help, doesn't know. Romeo waxes poetic about Juliet's beauty. He compares her to the torches, to a rich jewel and to a dove. Renouncing ever having loved before, he resolves to go near her and hold her hand. Tybalt recognizes the voice of a Montague and calls for his rapier. Capulet asks why Tybalt is angry. He responds that a Montague, their enemy, has come to mock them. Capulet recognizes Romeo and demands Tybalt settle down, pointing out that Romeo is behaving well and has a good reputation in Verona.

Tybalt says that he won't tolerate a Montague in the house. As master of the house, Capulet chides his nephew, saying he will cause a riot. When Tybalt resists further, Capulet calls him a "saucy boy" and says that acting this way will get him into trouble. Capulet alternates between scolding Tybalt and speaking cheerfully to his guests. In an aside, Tybalt says that he will leave, but vows to punish this intrusion later.

In sharp contrast to this violence, Romeo takes Juliet's hand and speaks the first lines of the famous Pilgrim sonnet, considered by many the most romantic passage in all of theater. In alternating lines, Shakespeare puns on the name "Romeo' (meaning "Pilgrim") as the two lovers share the conceit that Juliet is a holy statue and Romeo a reverent pilgrim.

Romeo pushes the metaphor, asking Juliet to grant his prayer for a kiss, to which she agrees.

Juliet is called away to her mother by the Nurse. Romeo asks the Nurse the identity of Juliet's mother and learns she is Lady Capulet. Romeo bemoans this, saying he now owes his life to his enemy. Benvolio suggests they leave, since the festivities are nearly over, and Romeo agrees. Capulet urges them to stay, but they gracefully decline.

As the guests are leaving, Juliet asks the Nurse the identity of each, covertly trying to find out Romeo's name. Juliet learns this from the Nurse and discovers he is a Montague. She laments, leaving together with the Nurse.

SONNET
The tightly controlled, highly structured poetic form of the Elizabethan Sonnet did constant battle against its desperately sentimental metaphors. Shakespeare exploited its volatile potentiality as the perfect medium to express the thunderbolt of Romeo and Juliet's first encounter.

ACT 2, SCENE 1

The Prologue; Romeo hides from Benvolio and Mercutio.

THE PROLOGUE OPENS with a metaphor for Romeo's emotional condition. It describes Romeo's past infatuation for Rosaline as an ailing patient, weak and wavering on its deathbed. At the foot of the bed stands the eager heir to Romeo's affections—his newfound love for Juliet. Rosaline, whose beauty Romeo extolled earlier in the play, cannot compare in loveliness to Juliet. Most importantly, the prologue continues, Romeo's love is now requited.

Romeo and Juliet are mutually enthralled by the sight of one another, but to Romeo's misfortune, he is now in love with a sworn enemy of his family. Because of this, Romeo must see Juliet under the threat of great danger to them both. What's more, Romeo does not have the access to Juliet that a lover would have under normal circumstances and thus is hindered in his wooing. Juliet is even more encumbered. In spite of all these obstacles, however, their passion empowers them and the joy of their meetings lessens the pain of their adversity.

Act 2, Scene 1 finds Romeo outside the Capulet orchard, deciding to follow his heart—which is to say, turn back and find Juliet. Mercutio and Benvolio enter, calling for Romeo and conversing in quick, monosyllabic lines. As there is no stage direction for Romeo's exit, often directors have Romeo crouch in hiding as he overhears his friends' conversation. Mercutio is convinced that Romeo has wisely gone home to bed. Benvolio believes that Romeo has leapt the orchard wall and asks Mercutio to call for him again. The diction becomes more elaborate as Mercutio playfully pretends to be a sorcerer. Believing Romeo is still in love with Rosaline, he conjurs Romeo by her beauty—her bright eyes, high forehead, scarlet lip and quivering thigh. Benvolio tells Mercutio to be quiet, saying he'll anger Romeo with this talk, should he overhear them. Not to be sensored, Mercutio persists and turns bawdy with a metaphor of raising spirits in his mistress' "circle."

Benvolio suggests that he and Mercutio leave, since apparently Romeo has hidden himself among the orchard trees. Picking up on this, Mercutio jokes that Romeo is probably sitting under a medlar tree, dreaming its fruit were Rosaline (medlar fruit resembles the female anatomy). He says the orchard is too cold and he would rather go home to his warm bed. Bemvolio agrees and resigns himself to leave, since Romeo obviously doesn't want to be found.

CHORUS
In late classical Greek dramatic tradition, a chorus was used as a detached, nonaligned commentary on the action of a play. In contrast to soliloquy, Shakespeare uses the prologue here as a *third-person* commentary on a character's innermost thoughts and feelings.

ACT 2, SCENE 2

The confession of love at Juliet's balcony; the agreement to marry.

ALONE IN THE Capulet orchard, Romeo remarks that Mercutio can only joke about love, having never experienced it. He breaks off his thought when he spies Juliet alone on her balcony. Romeo then speaks words of such stunning lyricism that western literature looks to this scene as the paean of love. In hyperbole, Romeo thinks of Juliet as the rising sun, shaming the moon. He sees that she is talking to herself, but he cannot make out her words.

Against the backdrop of Mercutio's vulgarity in the previous scene, Romeo forms poetic comparisons: Juliet's face is brighter than the stars; her eyes would light up the night; he longs to be a glove that touches her cheek—all typical Petrarchan metaphors. She sighs and he pines anew, imagining her to be an angel. Juliet speaks her famous monologue beginning, "O Romeo, Romeo, wherefore art thou Romeo?" (meaning, "Why are you Romeo?"). She dwells on the obstacle of their family names, asking rhetorically for Romeo to renounce his name and take all her love.

Romeo steps out of the shadows and speaks to her, vowing that if she loves him he will indeed forsake his name. She is startled and asks who is listening to her in the darkness. Romeo answers that he cannot tell her, since his name is her enemy and he now despises it. Juliet then recognizes Romeo's voice and asks why he has come. Romeo tells her that love has brought him. She warns him repeatedly that he will be killed if her family finds him on the Capulet grounds. Romeo says his only fear is that she will not return his love, saying, ironically, he would rather die.

Juliet asks him how he found her. He answers that love was his pilot and would have led him to her even if they were separated by oceans.

Juliet says she doesn't regret declaring her love for Romeo, although she blushes at being overheard earlier and decorum dictates she should deny her words. She cautions Romeo not to mistake the quick surrender of her affection for shallow infatuation.

When Romeo tries to swear his love by the moon, she says that the moon is inconstant and tells him to swear by himself, the object of her worship. She says good night between interruptions by the Nurse, who calls for her from inside. Romeo and Juliet make arrangements for their marriage the following day: Juliet will send a messenger to Romeo tomorrow who will send word of the arrangements back to Juliet. They part and Romeo resolves to go to Friar Lawrence for help.

CONCERNS
It is interesting to note that while other characters are concerned with the details of Romeo's whereabouts ("Where are you Romeo?"), Juliet is preoccupied with the essence of Romeo's identity ("Why are you Romeo?").

ACT 2, SCENE 3

Romeo asks Friar Lawrence to perform the secret wedding.

THE BENEVOLENT FRIAR opens the scene with a beautiful morning soliloquy. It is a speech of optimism in which he pictures the sun brightening the world as it usurps the drunken night. A botanist, the friar is filling his basket with powerful herbs from which he will make beneficial medicines. He remarks that, like people, no plant on earth is so evil that it does not contain some good within it—and nothing is so good that it cannot be twisted to some vile use.

Romeo calls to the friar and is greeted warmly, although Friar Lawrence believes that Romeo, a young man, must be full of worry to awaken so early in the morning—or possibly, he reasons, Romeo stayed up all night carousing. Romeo confirms the latter judgement, claiming his night was too sweet to allow him sleep. Friar Lawrence guesses that Romeo was out all night with Rosaline, but Romeo answers that he no longer loves her. When pressed further, Romeo speaks in generalities of "feasting with his enemy." He says that both of them now need the friar's good medicine.

Friar Lawrence urges Romeo to speak more plainly, telling him that riddles only bring about confusion. Romeo acquiesces; he tells Friar Lawrence of his mutually requited love for Capulet's daughter and their desire for the friar to marry them that very day.

Shocked, Friar Lawrence exclaims his skepticism at the sudden transfer of Romeo's affections. He claims Romeo is simply being led by his eyes, not by his heart. He reminds Romeo that he had seen him pining with tears and sighs for Rosaline only yesterday. The friar believes Romeo's emotions are too fickle. He asks him to repeat a sentence which essentially means, "Women succumb to the moral weakness of men."

Romeo protests, saying the friar admonished him for loving Rosaline. Friar Lawrence qualifies that he scolded him for *doting,* not for *loving* Rosaline. Echoing the chorus' deathbed metaphor, Romeo claims that the friar told him to bury his love for Rosaline. Friar Lawrence extends Romeo's image with a chilling image of his own, saying he did not instruct Romeo to place one corpse in the grave only to pluck another out.

Exasperated, Romeo says that Juliet returns his love, while Rosaline did not. The friar says Rosaline knew his love was mechanical and not heartfelt. However, he agrees to help Romeo and Juliet because it may end the bitter feud between the rival families Romeo's spirits soar as he and the friar leave to make plans.

MEDIATOR
Friar Lawrence is the only adult in the play who Romeo and Juliet enlist on their side. As such, he functions as a mediator between the pragmatic world of the adults and the idealistic world of the adolescents. Sadly, his mediation cannot succeed in bridging the gulf between the two dissimilar worlds.

ACT 2, SCENE 4

Mercutio's banter with Romeo; Romeo sends word to Juliet.

MERCUTIO ASKS BENVOLIO if Romeo came home last night. Benvolio says Romeo's servant told him he did not. Mercutio believes that Rosaline will drive Romeo to insanity. Switching the subject, Benvolio informs Mercutio that a letter from Tybalt was delivered to Montague, which Mercutio suspects is a challenge. Benvolio believes Romeo will answer the challenge, but Mercutio—with bawdy images—says Romeo has already been killed by Rosaline with Cupid's arrow.

Mercutio goes on to say that, this being the case, Romeo will be in no condition to encounter Tybalt. Benvolio asks why Mercutio believes Tybalt is so fearsome and Mercutio answers in a longwinded, satirical speech extolling Tybalt's "virtues." He begins by saying that Tybalt is far more than the Prince of Cats (punning on *Tibert,* a well-known fairy-tale cat). He then paints a picture of Tybalt as a polite swordsman who has been educated at the finest Italian fencing schools: he duels with textbook precision, but is more worried about what is fashionable than what is necessary in a fight.

Romeo enters and Mercutio makes jokes about him being sexually spent, then chides him for his absence. Romeo apologizes and says the business that occupied him was important. Attempting to reintegrate Romeo into their circle, he goads him into a battle of words. Romeo, picking up on Mercutio's intention, eventually joins in and the result is a quick and wonderful wordplay between the two friends, fraught with Elizabethan colloquialisms.

Words are thrown out as challenges and the banter moves from one to the next—pink, sole, goose—at the whim of the participants. Mercutio stops the contest, asking Romeo to admit that this male bonding is better than lovesickness.

The Nurse enters, attended by Peter. Mercutio makes fun of her clothing and begins a string of lewd jokes. The Nurse asks for Romeo and—after Mercutio finally stops his indecent jokes and exits with Benvolio—the two confer about plans for him to marry Juliet that evening.

The Nurse tiresomely misinterprets Romeo's speech, but eventually arrives at the correct understanding: he wishes to marry Juliet in honorable fashion. He says that Juliet should tell her family she's going to confession at the friar's that afternoon. After paying the Nurse for carrying the message, he continues that he will have a servant bring her a rope ladder to set out so Romeo may be with Juliet for their wedding night. They part quickly, both in high spirits.

WIT
The verbal contest between the two friends is a demonstration of theatrical wit—the combination of humor and intelligence used to hallmark a character's cleverness. Mercutio assigns this witty banter as an intrinsic element of Romeo's nature, attempting to end his self-imposed banishment from their clique.

ACT 2, SCENE 5

The Nurse keeps Juliet in suspense before telling the news from Romeo.

JULIET PACES IMPATIENTLY as she awaits the Nurse's return from her errand. She remarks that it was nine o'clock in the morning when she sent the Nurse to Romeo. At noon there is still no sign of her return. In soliloquy, Juliet compares the passionate motivations of youth with the unimpassioned sluggishness of adults. She says that if the Nurse were young, she would be as a ball that Juliet and Romeo could lovingly toss back and forth to each other.

The Nurse finally arrives and Juliet rushes to meet her, asking what news she brings from Romeo. At Juliet's request, the Nurse tells Peter to wait by the gate. Juliet then asks why the Nurse looks so sad, thinking that the news she brings must surely match her countenance. She begs the Nurse to tell her good news, whether it truly is good or bad, and she chides the Nurse for spoiling her beautiful moment with such a sour face. The Nurse is in no hurry and keeps Juliet in suspense, complaining of aching feet and asking Juliet to let her catch her breath.

Juliet grumbles that if the Nurse were really out of breath, she wouldn't be able complain about her condition. She compromises her request, asking simply that the Nurse tell her whether the news is good or bad—being satisfied to know the details later.

The Nurse chides Juliet for her choice of Romeo, even though she admits he is an extraordinarily handsome man, and tells her to go serve God instead. Veering off topic, she asks Juliet if she has eaten yet. Frustrated, Juliet answers that she has not and she asks the Nurse directly what Romeo said about the wedding. Prolonging the suspense, the Nurse switches the subject to complaints about her head and back. She curses Juliet

for sending her across town on her errand. Juliet apologizes and begs the Nurse again to answer her question and tell her what Romeo said about their wedding plans.

In a final skirting of the issue, the Nurse begins to answer Juliet to the point and suddenly stops, asking where Lady Capulet is at the moment. Beyond patience, Juliet tells her Lady Capulet is inside and then berates her for such an odd reply.

The Nurse finally tells Juliet the news: Romeo is waiting to marry her in Friar Lawrence's chamber. The Nurse was given a further errand by Romeo to bring a ladder by which he'll climb to Juliet's room that evening. Juliet is overjoyed at the news and the Nurse hurries her off to her wedding.

PHYSICAL
This scene is usually played with Juliet touching the Nurse a great deal in an attempt to pacify her complaints and extract the import of Romeo's message. For example, Juliet will rub the Nurse's aching feet and switch to rubbing her throbbing temples in time with the Nurse's shifting afflictions.

ACT 2, SCENE 6

Romeo and Juliet are married in Friar Lawrence's chamber.

THIS VERY SHORT SCENE marks the play's optimistic zenith. Amid the destructive violence of the feud and the stressful urgency of the prohibited relationship, the audience is privy to a parenthesis where no condemning adult threatens to intrude and the love between Romeo and Juliet can be expressed. Friar Lawrence, as ever, stands as mediator between the idealistic adolescents and the adult world, attempting to usher them into legitimacy with the clandestine sacrament.

The scene opens with a benediction from Friar Lawrence, asking for God's blessing on the forthcoming "holy act" as he and Romeo await the arrival of Juliet. Romeo affirms the prayer, but tells the friar that even if sorrow should come upon them afterward—using the term "love-devouring death"—it is enough for him that he should be able to call Juliet his wife. Friar Lawrence cautions Romeo that such passionate feelings can bring about passionate consequences. He instructs Romeo to love with moderation, which he believes will ensure love's survival.

The friar sees Juliet approaching and segues into the theme of lasting love, waxing rapsodic about the lightness that love has placed in Juliet's step.

Juliet arrives and greets the friar as her "ghostly confessor." The term (first used by Romeo in 2.1) has a myriad of resonances. As "spiritual advisor to overhear the confession of my sins," it is a reminder that Juliet is there under the pretense of shrift, reinforcing the clandestine nature of their wedding. As "spiritual advisor to overhear the confession of my love," it points to the forbidden nature of her love for Romeo. Finally, it hints at "deathbed confessor," which forshadows the impending doom that both lovers will share by play's end.

Friar Lawrence says that Romeo will greet her for both of them, meaning that Romeo will kiss her, which he does. Juliet says that she will return Romeo's thanks and she kisses him again. Romeo, finding inspiration in Juliet's kisses, asks her to to put her thoughts into words, calling for her to "let rich music's tongue" reveal to him if her happiness is truly as great as his. Juliet responds in poetic kind. She says words are poor vehicles for the real love she is experiencing at that moment. The riches of her love, she continues, have grown so huge that she cannot reckon half of their wealth. The friar interrupts this heartfelt exchange to remind them they must first be wed and they exit to perform the ceremony.

EXCHANGES
It is thematic for Juliet to return whatever commodity is implied to have been imparted by Romeo's kiss. In this scene, the commodity is thanks. At the moment of their first kiss in 1.5, the commodity was sin. In their final kiss, the commodity will be death.

ACT 3, SCENE 1

Tybalt slays Mercutio; Romeo slays Tybalt; Romeo is banished.

ONLY AN HOUR LATER, on the hot summer afternoon of their marriage, Benvolio and Mercutio are talking outside. Benvolio urges him to go inside, since the Capulets are about and there will be no way to avoid a fight should they meet. Mercutio says Benvolio has no right to speak of quarrels and he teasingly describes Benvolio as a ruffian who would quarrel with a man for trivial reasons (several of which he lists to the delight of the audience).

As Mercutio and Benvolio trade witticisms, Tybalt approaches looking for Romeo. He asks to have a word with one of them and Mercutio begins goading him for a fight. Tybalt says he'll be happy to fight and Mercutio has an easy task of verbal gaming at Tybalt's expense. Benvolio entreats them to discuss their differences in private, but neither man agrees. Romeo enters and Tybalt's agression shifts to its original target. He clumsily insults Romeo. Romeo—elated from his wedding—excuses the insult and tells Tybalt that he feels only love toward him.

Mercutio, enraged by Romeo's passive response, draws on Tybalt and the two enemies fight. Romeo attempts to come between them and when he does, Tybalt thrusts under Romeo's arm, wounding Mercutio, and then exits.

Benvolio and Romeo go to help Mercutio, who sends his servant for a doctor. Despite Romeo's attempts at encouragement, Mercutio soon realizes he is dying and he pronounces the famous curse: "A plague o'both your houses."

Benvolio helps Mercutio inside and Romeo speaks a short soliloquy in which he claims Juliet's love has made him soft and effeminate. Benvolio quickly reappears to give the news that Mercutio is dead.

Romeo believes Mercutio's death is but the beginning of sorrow. Tybalt reenters and Romeo confronts him, telling him to take back his earlier insult. Tybalt refuses and they fight, with Romeo the eventual victor. Benvolio tells Romeo to run away for his own safety and he complies.

The prince appears along with the heads of the Montague and Capulet houses. At the prince's request Benvolio explains what happened. Lady Capulet calls Benvolio a liar, pointing out his relation to Romeo. She calls for Romeo's death. The prince reminds Lady Capulet that Romeo slew Tybalt to avenge the death of Mercutio (the prince's kinsman). Not wishing to condone violence, however, the prince banishes Romeo from Verona.

BANISHMENT
Banishment is the forced expulsion of a person from a country by official decree (as opposed to *exile,* which connotes voluntary departure). In cases where capital punishment was unwarranted, the state often preferred it to life imprisonment because of its relative economy.

ACT 3, SCENE 2

The Nurse tells Juliet the news of Romeo's banishment.

SHORTLY BEFORE NIGHTFALL, only three hours after her wedding, Juliet waits anxiously for the sun to set, bringing darkness to conceal Romeo's journey to her bedchamber. In poetic soliloquy, Juliet blurs three primary metaphors: anthropomorphized night; herself a trembling, hooded bird of prey waiting for her hunter; and Romeo scattered into the night sky as stars shaming the sun. Her tone is restless—she describes herself as an impatient child the night before a holiday.

The Nurse enters, carrying a rope ladder and wringing her hands. Juliet asks her if the rope ladder is from Romeo and she answers distractedly. Then Juliet asks the Nurse why she looks so distraught and the Nurse answers, "...he's dead, he's dead, he's dead!" (speaking of Tybalt). Juliet misinterprets the Nurse to mean Romeo is dead and they have a disjointed conversation—halfway through, Juliet thinks Romeo and Tybalt are both dead—until the Nurse clarifies that Romeo has killed Tybalt and has been banished by the prince.

Juliet launches into a surprisingly uncharacteristic, oxymoron-riddled attack on Romeo, calling him a snake, dragon, devil, raven, wolf and villain. She laments that she was deceived by his beauty. The Nurse, after calling for Peter to bring her a brandy, joins in with Juliet. She describes all men as good-for-nothing liars and pronounces shame on Romeo.

Hearing the nurse curse Romeo brings about a change of heart in Juliet. She chides the nurse for wishing Romeo any ill-will and admits she was wrong to have spoken that way herself about him.

The Nurse is surprised by Juliet's attitude and asks her how she can speak well of her cousin's murderer.

Juliet asks how the Nurse expects her to speak ill of her own husband. She realizes that Tybalt would have killed Romeo, had Romeo not killed him first. She wonders why she is weeping and then remembers that Romeo has been banished. She describes this punishment as worse than death. She asks the Nurse the whereabouts of her mother and father. The Nurse answers that they are mourning Tybalt and says she can take Juliet to them. Deeply grieving, Juliet says she can only go to her bed and die a widowed maiden.

The Nurse comforts Juliet, saying she will find Romeo and tell him to go to Juliet that night as planned. At this, Juliet brightens and gives the Nurse a ring to give to him.

ROLLER-COASTER
More so than any other scene, 3.2 is the emotional pinion around which the play turns. Juliet is its unwitting center as she moves from restless expectancy to rage, betrayal, apology, depression and finally, hope.

ACT 3, SCENE 3

Romeo's suicide prevented; the friar and Nurse lift Romeo's spirits.

FRIAR LAWRENCE ENTERS his room and speaks to Romeo, who is in hiding. He tells Romeo that the prince has imposed the merciful sentence of banishment instead of capital punishment. Romeo groans and says he would rather have been killed. He compares Verona to heaven, since Juliet is there, and claims the rest of the world is either tortuous purgatory or damnable hell. He says that Friar Lawrence has smilingly cut off his head with a golden axe.

The Friar scolds Romeo for his ungratefulness. He says the prince has shown rare mercy by commuting his sentence to banishment. Romeo argues that the friar would have a different opinion if he could exchange places with Romeo—a young man, newly married to a loving wife and banished for murdering her kinsman. As they argue, there is a loud knocking at the door. Friar Lawrence tells Romeo to hide in the study, fearing he will be siezed by the authorities. Romeo refuses, too lethargic from his depression. The friar urges more forcefully and, once Romeo is safely hidden, answers the door.

It is the Nurse. She asks Friar Lawrence where she can find Romeo and the friar directs her to the floor, where Romeo lay weeping. The Nurse exclaims that he is in the identical condition of Juliet. She tells Romeo to stand up and stop blubbering, which he does. He asks how Juliet is handling the news and what she thinks of him now that he has murdered her cousin. The Nurse says Juliet does nothing but weep. Occasionally, she stands and calls alternately for Tybalt and Romeo, only to fall sobbing again.

Romeo says that his vile name has murdered his beloved and he grabs a dagger, threatening to cut out its essence from his body. Scholars are divided as to who actually disarms Romeo, although the consensus leans toward the Nurse. In either case, Romeo's suicide attempt is stayed. Friar Lawrence delivers a stern sermon to Romeo, calling his tears womanish, his thoughless behavior beastly, and his suicide attempt damnable. He reminds Romeo that Juliet is still alive and that the murder of Tybalt was done in self-defense. He counsels Romeo to see Juliet tonight as planned, then go live in Mantua until the friar has opportunity to announce the marriage, reconcile the families and beg pardon of the prince.

The Nurse leaves after giving Romeo Juliet's ring. The friar promises to send word to Romeo through his servant and Romeo departs for Juliet with a renewed hope.

NAMES
Thematically, Romeo focuses his hatred on his name—in this scene asking Friar Lawrence where it resides in his body so he can excise it with his dagger. This preoccupation with identity is unique to Shakespeare's version.

ACT 3, SCENE 4

Capulet promises Juliet to Paris and sets the wedding for Thursday.

LATE MONDAY NIGHT, the night of Juliet's wedding, the same hour that Romeo and Juliet are in her room consummating their nuptials, Capulet and Paris are in the Capulet household discussing the progress of Juliet's interest in the count. Feeling himself in an inferior position in the negotiations owing to his neglect to speak with Juliet at any length, Capulet's tone is apologetic and garrulous against the ever laconic Paris.

Capulet begins by explaining his reason for not yet speaking with Juliet: the unfortunate death of Tybalt has placed certain obligations of mourning upon his household. These funereal obligations have not allowed sufficient time for talk of marriage. He follows this explanation with the maxim: "Well, we were born to die," perhaps in an attempt to normalize the violence surrounding his family. He continues, saying Juliet cannot join them—because of the lateness of the hour—pointing out that he, himself, would be in bed were it not for Paris' company.

Paris politely asks Lady Capulet to give his regards to Juliet before excusing himself. Lady Capulet agrees and tells Paris she will know the next day Juliet's intent toward his suit for marriage.

The remainder of this scene is the emotional downturn of the play. The Q1 stage direction: *Paris offers to go in and Capulet calls him again,* is simple enough, but Capulet's change in heart can sometimes seem unmotivated. Often, a director will have Lady Capulet cast a stern glance at her husband, nodding quickly in Paris' direction as if to say, "Don't let this one get away!" In any case, the gesture is unnecessary when we consider Capulet's shrinking net worth (he has just lost a valuable investment in Tybalt), his

ostensible loss of patriarchal authority (Paris often helps make this clear to the audience by raising his eyebrows, insinuating his belief that Juliet is calling the shots in the Capulet family) and his genuine concern for both his family's and Juliet's financial well being (which marrying her to a kinsman of the prince would certainly further).

Capulet rashly agrees to the marriage, saying Juliet will abide by his wishes. He asks Lady Capulet to inform Juliet before she goes to bed. Ignoring his earlier two-year waiting period, he hastily sets the date of the marriage for Thursday and cautions that it should be a small celebration, so as not to violate protocol for the recent funeral. Believing all is settled, he says goodnight to Paris and goes to bed.

AUTHORITY
The idea of patriarchal ownership of sons and daughters was ingrained in Elizabethan culture. Sir Robert Filmer's *Patriarcha* (1680), developed the argument that this authority was handed down from the biblical patriarchs and was, conveniently, thus ordained by God.

ACT 3, SCENE 5

The Aubade; Juliet is horrified by news of her impending marriage.

Morning brings the demand of Romeo's departure. The newlyweds engage in an emotionally desperate conversation wherein Juliet pretends it is not yet day. She tries to convince Romeo they heard a nightingale singing, rather than a lark. Romeo resignedly and tenderly points out the realities of daybreak: the streaks of sunlight, the absence of stars. Juliet continues to defend her invention, saying the sun is but a meteor in the night and therefore Romeo has time to stay.

Romeo concedes, joining Juliet in her make-believe, saying that if Juliet wills it, he would rather stay with her and die than depart and live. At the mention of Romeo's possible death, Juliet snaps out of her fantasy and insists that he leave, blaming the lark's song for parting them. The Nurse calls from within, warning Juliet that her mother is coming. After a farewell kiss, Romeo descends the balcony. Juliet implores him to write every hour. She remarks that Romeo has the appearance of a dead man descending into a tomb. He says she appears likewise to him since sorrow is draining them both of life.

Lady Capulet enters and—thinking Juliet cries for Tybalt—she scolds her daughter, reminding her that moderate grief is loving, while excessive grief is foolish. Lady Capulet believes that Romeo's life is the true source of Juliet's grief (because he is Tybalt's murderer). In duplicitous responses, Juliet heartily agrees, but for antithetical reasons. Interpreting Juliet's answers as vengeful passion, Lady Capulet says she will send someone to Mantua to poison Romeo. Juliet says she'll mix the poison herself, so Romeo will sleep quietly.

To brighten the mood, Lady Capulet tells Juliet her father has arranged her marriage to Paris. Juliet says to tell her father she would rather marry Tybalt's murderer than Paris.

Capulet enters and Lady Capulet tells him that Juliet is against the arranged marriage. Hearing this, Capulet moves from confused to furious. He insults Juliet, threatens to hit her (the Nurse intervenes) and finally vows to disown her if she will not marry. After he exits, Juliet begs her mother to delay the marriage. Lady Capulet declines and follows her husband.

Juliet turns to the Nurse, asking for advice and comfort. The Nurse counsels her to submit to the marriage, since Romeo is gone forever. She then extols the virtues of Paris over Romeo. Juliet— secretly enraged at the Nurse—asks her to tell Lady Capulet she is going to Friar Lawrence to confess her sin of disobedience. Juliet leaves, resolving to kill herself if necessary.

ABANDONMENT
In this scene, Juliet is abandoned by all those she loves. First, we see Romeo leave, albeit against his will. Her father vows to disown her. Her mother sides with him. And, finally, she is alone as the Nurse counsels her to betray her love for Romeo.

ACT 4, SCENE 1

Juliet unexpectedly encounters Paris; the friar devises a desperate plan.

LATER THAT MORNING, in Friar Lawrence's room, Paris informs the friar that the date of his wedding to Juliet has been expedited to Thursday. Friar Lawrence is disturbed by the haste and he voices his concern. Paris counters with the argument that Juliet's father believes the wedding will be a cure for his daughter's excessive grief over Tybalt. In an aside, Friar Lawrence laments the real reason for his concern: he has already married Juliet to Romeo.

Juliet enters on her way to confession and Paris is excited at the unexpected meeting. He greets her as his "lady" and "wife." Juliet resists the titles, saying they are too soon applied. In the ensuing conversation, Paris tries to establish his ownership of her and pressures her to say that she loves him. She rebuffs him with brilliant language that is both respectful and firm. Juliet dismisses Paris by asking the friar if he is available to hear her confession. Friar Lawrence entreats Paris to leave and he obliges. Paris kisses Juliet politely (on the hand or forehead in most performances) and exits.

Juliet asks Friar Lawrence to weep with her, as her situation appears hopeless. The friar says he already knows the reason for her sorrow (the expedited wedding date) but is unable to discern a solution. Juliet responds with a plea for him to not even speak of the wedding unless it is to tell her how to prevent it.

In her desperation, Juliet produces a knife. She vows she will commit suicide before allowing either her heart or her hand to betray Romeo. Seeking an honorable way out of her predicament, she asks to be the benefactor of either the friar's experience or the knife's remedy. Friar Lawrence says that if Juliet is courageous enough to kill herself, then he has a solution that is almost as extreme as suicide.

Juliet's spirits are lifted as she confesses the valor of her love. She claims she would rather live with snakes, hide in a graveyard or be buried alive for the privilege of living with Romeo. Convinced, the friar hands her a vial and tells her his plan. Alone on Wednesday night, she is to drink this sleeping potion, which will cause her to appear dead for forty-two hours. Her family will find her lifeless on the morning of her wedding day. They will grieve and then bury her in the Capulet tomb. He and Romeo will hide inside, waiting for her to awake, after which she and Romeo will flee to Mantua.

Juliet agrees and, as they part, Friar Lawrence tells her he will arrange for a fellow friar to carry a letter to Romeo, telling him of their plan.

DEVICE
Shakespeare alters his source by adding the encounter between Paris and Juliet at Friar Lawrence's chamber. This device serves to increase Juliet's resolve, show Juliet's character development (she is much stronger than when we first meet her) and makes real the impending arranged marriage.

ACT 4, SCENES 2 & 3

Wedding preparations; Juliet's repentance; she drinks the potion.

LATE TUESDAY AFTERNOON finds the Capulet household in a flurry of wedding preparations. Capulet sends a servant to invite the guests. He sends another servant to hire twenty of the best cooks. That servant responds in low-comic fashion, saying he will put the cooks to a test: if they will not lick their own fingers, then he will not hire them. Capulet hurries the servant on his way, telling him to make haste or the preparations will not be finished in time.

Capulet confirms with the Nurse that Juliet has gone to Friar Lawrence's for confession. He expresses his hope that the friar will have a positive effect on her peevish stubbornness. Juliet returns with a happier expression. Capulet, still skeptical, calls her "my headstrong" and asks her where she has been in a way that assumes she has been up to no good. Juliet says she has repented of her sin of disobedience. She kneels before her father and begs his forgiveness. While her contrition does not alter her heartfelt commitment to be with Romeo, she does, nevertheless, genuinely regret angering her father.

Capulet is overcome by the gesture and he asks for Paris to be brought. Juliet tells her father that she has just spoken with Paris at Friar Lawrence's and says she was as loving to him as modesty would allow. Beaming, Capulet bids Juliet rise. He calls for a servant to bring Paris to him. He extols Friar Lawrence, saying the city of Verona is much indebted to him.

Juliet asks the Nurse to help her find the appropriate clothes for the next day. When Lady Capulet points out that the wedding is actually two days away on Thursday, Capulet moves the date forward to Wednesday. Lady Capulet protests, saying the provisions will not be finished, but Capulet says he will stay up all night to make sure they are. In his excitement, he leaves to walk to the home of Paris.

Once in her bedroom, Juliet dismisses her mother and the Nurse (she begins to call them back, but stops). Then, in her longest soliloquy, Juliet prepares to drink the sleeping potion. She considers several possible mishaps: what if the drug fails and she must marry tomorrow (she lays a knife by her bed, just in case); what if the friar actually gave her a poison to cover up his own dishonor (she finds no evidence to support this); what if she awakens early in the tomb and either suffocates or goes mad and beats herself to death with a kinsman's bones (this truly terrifies her).

Juliet hallucinates, seeing her cousin Tybalt's ghost searching for Romeo. She yells wildly for him to stop. She then calls to Romeo, drinks the potion and collapses on the bed.

TRIBUTE
At the end of this scene, Juliet utters a toast to Romeo before drinking the friar's sleeping potion. This tribute prefigures Romeo's "Here's to my love!" in 5.3 before he drinks the apothecary's poison, ending his life. In both cases, the lovers invoke the source of their strength—their love for each other.

ACT 4, SCENES 4 & 5

More arrangements; Juliet is found and presumed dead; Peter's quarrel.

IT IS THREE in the morning as the Capulet household works energetically on the final wedding arrangements, echoing the opening of 4.2. Lady Capulet asks the Nurse to fetch spices and Capulet asks her to make sure there is enough meat as well. The Nurse playfully calls him a cotquean—a "househusband"—and sends him to bed. He resists, saying he has stayed up many a night without consequence. Lady Capulet jokes that he did so only when he was womanizing.

Servants enter with logs and baskets for the cooks. Capulet directs one of them to consult Peter where drier wood may be found. The servant answers in clown-like fashion, saying essentially that he'll find the logs himself because his head is made of wood. Capulet delights in the wordplay, but stiffens as the sound of music is heard in the distance. He remarks that it is nearly daylight and Paris must be arriving with the musicians. He tells the Nurse to quickly wake Juliet and help her to dress for the wedding while he chats with Paris.

In Juliet's room, the Nurse tries to awaken her for some thirteen lines. She makes a bawdy joke about how Paris will keep her up all night once they're married. She laughs to herself and then notes that Juliet is still in her clothes.

Upon finding Juliet "dead," the Nurse calls frantically for Lord and Lady Capulet. They enter and grieve with the Nurse about the untimely loss of their only daughter.

Friar Lawrence enters with Paris (and perhaps the musicians). The friar plays dumb, asking if Juliet is ready for church. Capulet answers that she is, but for a funeral instead of a wedding. Capulet turns to Paris and proclaims Death has beaten him to Juliet, deflowering her on the night before

her wedding. Lady Capulet, the Nurse and Capulet trade outbursts of grief before Friar Lawrence admonishes them. He advises them not to grieve more than is natural, since Juliet is now happily in heaven. He directs them to drape her in flowers and carry her to church.

After they exit, the musicians decide to leave, but Peter enters and requests they play a traditional, lively dirge. They decline, saying now is no time for music. Using musical metaphors, Peter threatens to beat and stab them, thus beginning an argument reminiscent of the servant's quarrel in 1.1. Peter then tells the musicians they won't be paid and exits. After calling him a rogue, the musicians decide to wait for the mourners and stay for dinner.

DEATH
Capulet uses the motif of Death as Juliet's bridegroom, the usurper of Paris' marital privileges. In doing so, he paints a macabre epitaph that will be revisited by Romeo in 5.3.

ACT 5, SCENES 1 & 2

The news of Juliet's "death"; Romeo buys poison; the undelivered letter.

LATER THAT DAY, the day of Juliet's funeral, the exiled Romeo muses about a strange and extraordinary dream he had the night before. He intimates that his heart is light because he believes this dream foretells good news—Romeo dreamed he was dead and Juliet's kisses resurrected him to a new life as an emperor. Romeo comments that love shared between two people must be sweet indeed since a mere dream of love can be so wondrous.

Romeo's servant, Balthazar, enters and Romeo barrages him with questions about his loved ones. He exclaims that nothing can be wrong as long as Juliet is well. Balthazar says she sleeps well in the Capulet tomb and her soul lives well with the angels. He apologizes for the unfortunate news, telling Romeo he left on horseback immediately after seeing Juliet's body placed in the family tomb. Romeo curses his fate. He tells Balthazar to bring ink and paper to his room and to hire horses for travel that night. Balthazar begs Romeo to have patience seeing that his looks are wild and portend calamity.

Romeo reassures him and asks him a second time if he carries letters from Friar Lawrence. Balthazar answers that he does not, so Romeo dismisses him to complete his errands.

Walking through Mantua, Romeo reveals in soliloquy his intention to commit suicide next to Juliet's body in the Capulet tomb. He recalls seeing a destitute apothecary (a druggist) and thinking that if anyone was in need of poison—the sale of which amounted to a capital offense in Mantua—then certainly this was the man to sell it. Resolving to fulfill that prophetic memory, Romeo calls out to the apothecary, whose shop is closed for an unnamed holiday. The apothecary appears and Romeo offers him forty ducats for a small bottle of poison. Though afraid of the threat of capital punishment for selling poison, the destitute apothecary is easily convinced to take the money. He warns Romeo that the poison is powerful enough to kill twenty men. Romeo hands him the money and rushes off to die at Juliet's side.

5.2 opens as Friar John tells Friar Lawrence of his unsuccessful attempt to deliver the letter to Romeo. Friar John says he sought a fellow Franciscan, who he found visiting a house of the sick, as a travel companion. Sadly, both friars were then quarantined to ensure they were not infected with the plague. Alarmed, Friar Lawrence sends Friar John to fetch a crowbar. He plans to greet the awakening Juliet and take her to his room, where he will send word to Romeo and await his arrival.

PLAGUE
Mercutio's dying curse in 3.1, "A plague o' both your houses!" comes true with the quarantine of the friars. The plague literally becomes the decisive hindrance to Friar Lawrence's message to Romeo, thereby triggering the chain of events culminating in the destruction of the heirs of both houses.

ACT 5, SCENE 3 PART 1

At Juliet's grave, Romeo reluctantly kills Paris, then drinks the poison.

THE LONGEST SCENE of the play opens late at night with Paris and his page at the Capulet tomb. He orders the page to stand watch at a distance and whistle if anyone approaches. Paris scatters flowers over the tomb and grieves for his dead betrothed, promising to visit her grave each night. The page whistles and Paris quickly hides. Romeo enters with Balthazar, carrying a pick and crowbar. Romeo hands Balthazar a letter, telling him to deliver it to his father, Montague, in the morning.

Romeo tells Balthazar to leave and threatens to kill him if he returns. He invents a story that he has come to retrieve an expensive ring. He hands Balthazar money and says goodbye. Balthazar leaves, but decides to hide nearby, fearing Romeo's intentions. Thinking himself alone, Romeo pries open the tomb and resolves to die inside. Paris recognizes Romeo as the killer of Tybalt, the cousin of his beloved. Juliet's grief over Tybalt's murder, he believes, makes Romeo indirectly responsible for *her* death, as well. He thinks Romeo has come to desecrate their bodies.

Paris comes forward to arrest Romeo and have him put to death. In the darkness, Romeo does not recognize Paris. Romeo tells him that he has come to the tomb to die and warns him not to anger a desperate man. He points out the corpses inside the tomb in an attempt to scare Paris off.

Paris is unmoved. They fight. Seeing the commotion, the page runs to get the authorities. Paris is mortally wounded. As he dies, he asks to be laid with Juliet and Romeo agrees.

In the torchlight, Romeo finally recognizes Paris as Mercutio's kinsman who was to marry Juliet. Taking Paris' hand, he pronounces they have been bound together in mutual misfortune. Talking to the dead Paris, Romeo says he will bury him in a magnificent palace that is lighted by Juliet's beauty. He lays Paris down inside the tomb (nothing in the text indicates that Paris is laid next to Juliet).

Seeing Juliet laying in the tomb, Romeo speaks to her, remarking that death has not spoiled her beauty. Turning to Tybalt's body, Romeo asks his forgiveness and vows to end the life of his enemy, meaning himself. He returns to Juliet and asks if she is still so beautiful because Death is keeping her for his mistress. To guard against this, Romeo promises to stay with her in the tomb forever.

Taking a final embrace, he raises the vial of poison, calling it the captain of a doomed ship. Toasting his love, he drinks and dies quickly on Juliet's bosom.

IRONY
The highest act of love Romeo can achieve is death of self, hoping to form a lifeless, eternal unity with his Juliet. This ironic motif of death for love is driven by the necessity to freeze the lovers at their point of highest passion and yearning— the metaphor for which will be the golden statues, forged by the reconciliation of the houses.

ACT 5, SCENE 3 PART 2

Juliet awakens and joins Romeo in death; the families reconcile.

FRIAR LAWRENCE STUMBLES upon Balthazar near the tomb. The friar asks whose light is burning inside the vault and Balthazar tells him it belongs to Romeo. The friar then asks Balthazar to join him. He refuses, saying Romeo sent him away and swore to kill him if he stayed. Though afraid, Friar Lawrence decides to go in alone. Balthazar says he just dreamt Romeo killed a man in a fight. The friar enters the tomb to find Romeo and Paris dead: Romeo pale, Paris steeped in blood.

Juliet awakens. She is relieved to see Friar Lawrence. Perhaps still in a daze from the potion, she asks him where Romeo is. The friar urges her to leave with him, as he hears noise outside. He points out the two dead men—Paris nearby and Romeo in her lap. In desperation, he offers to hide Juliet in a convent. Hearing the watch approaching, the friar says they must leave immediately. Juliet vows to stay, but bids him go and he does. Alone, Juliet discovers the bottle in Romeo's hand and curses that none is left for her. Hoping some poison remains, on his lips, she kisses him and discovers his lips still warm.

Hearing the watch close by, Juliet says she must be quick. She takes Romeo's dagger and plunges it into her bosom. Outside, the page leads the watch to the tomb. Seeing blood on the ground, the first watchman initiates a search of the churchyard. Looking into the tomb, he sees the bodies of Juliet and Paris (Romeo is not mentioned, although the watchman apparently sees him as well). He gives orders to wake the Prince, Capulets and Montagues. The second watchman brings in Balthazar, who is held for the arrival of the prince. The third watchman brings in the friar, who he found weeping and trembling, carrying a pick and spade. He is held as well.

As dawn approaches, the prince arrives, demanding an explanation. Capulet and his wife arrive moments later. The watchman reports that Paris, Romeo and Juliet are dead. Seeing the bodies, Capulet says the dagger should be in Montague's back, rather than in his daughter's bosom. Lady Capulet feels her own death is near. Montague arrives and says his wife has died of grief over Romeo's exile.

The friar steps forward and relates the entire story of Romeo and Juliet's tragedy, accepting full responsibility for his part. Balthazar shows Romeo's letter to the prince, confirming the friar's story. The prince excuses the friar and admonishes both Capulet and Montague. Capulet offers his hand in friendship to Montague. In return, Montague promises to make a gold statue of Juliet. Capulet says he will make one of Romeo. The prince closes the play with a dark eulogy.

TRIUMPH
In the Prologue we are told that the deaths of Romeo and Juliet will "bury their parents' strife," which is to say, overcome the onerous stranglehold of hatred the feud has exercised over the two families. Only their children's transcendent act of dying for each other's love could bring about the triumphant reconciliation of the warring houses.

APPENDIX A:
DRAMATIC MAPS

The Dramatic Maps which follow are schematic representations of *Romeo and Juliet* by scene. In each case, the main ideas of the scene are highlighted on the timeline, alongside their initial corresponding line number. The brackets attempt larger groupings of the ideas to provide a sense of the overall movement of the scene. The line numbers of Shakespeare's *Romeo and Juliet* differ greatly between Quartos, Folios and, consequently, publishers—each publishing is an interpretive work. Keep in mind they are guidelines for general assistance; your specific version may vary.

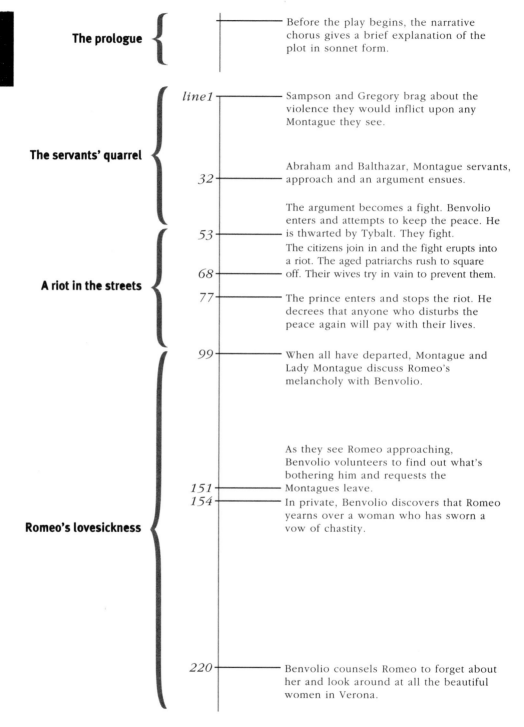

The prologue { Before the play begins, the narrative chorus gives a brief explanation of the plot in sonnet form.

line1 — Sampson and Gregory brag about the violence they would inflict upon any Montague they see.

The servants' quarrel {

32 — Abraham and Balthazar, Montague servants, approach and an argument ensues.

53 — The argument becomes a fight. Benvolio enters and attempts to keep the peace. He is thwarted by Tybalt. They fight.

68 — The citizens join in and the fight erupts into a riot. The aged patriarchs rush to square off. Their wives try in vain to prevent them.

A riot in the streets {

77 — The prince enters and stops the riot. He decrees that anyone who disturbs the peace again will pay with their lives.

99 — When all have departed, Montague and Lady Montague discuss Romeo's melancholy with Benvolio.

151 — As they see Romeo approaching, Benvolio volunteers to find out what's bothering him and requests the Montagues leave.

154 — In private, Benvolio discovers that Romeo yearns over a woman who has sworn a vow of chastity.

Romeo's lovesickness {

220 — Benvolio counsels Romeo to forget about her and look around at all the beautiful women in Verona.

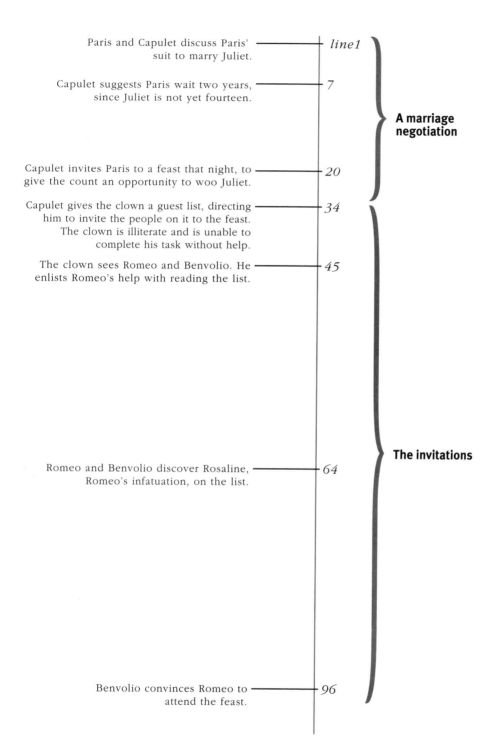

Paris and Capulet discuss Paris' suit to marry Juliet. — *line 1*

Capulet suggests Paris wait two years, since Juliet is not yet fourteen. — 7

A marriage negotiation

Capulet invites Paris to a feast that night, to give the count an opportunity to woo Juliet. — 20

Capulet gives the clown a guest list, directing him to invite the people on it to the feast. The clown is illiterate and is unable to complete his task without help. — 34

The clown sees Romeo and Benvolio. He enlists Romeo's help with reading the list. — 45

The invitations

Romeo and Benvolio discover Rosaline, Romeo's infatuation, on the list. — 64

Benvolio convinces Romeo to attend the feast. — 96

1.2

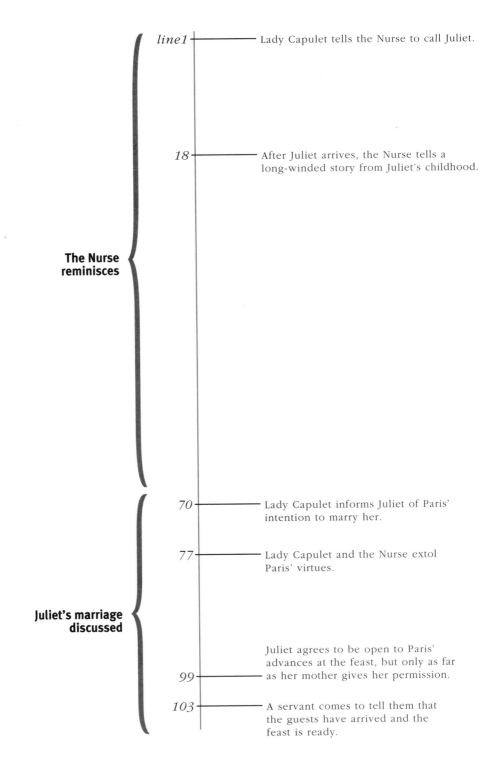

1.3

line1 ——— Lady Capulet tells the Nurse to call Juliet.

18 ——— After Juliet arrives, the Nurse tells a long-winded story from Juliet's childhood.

The Nurse reminisces

70 ——— Lady Capulet informs Juliet of Paris' intention to marry her.

77 ——— Lady Capulet and the Nurse extol Paris' virtues.

Juliet's marriage discussed

99 ——— Juliet agrees to be open to Paris' advances at the feast, but only as far as her mother gives her permission.

103 ——— A servant comes to tell them that the guests have arrived and the feast is ready.

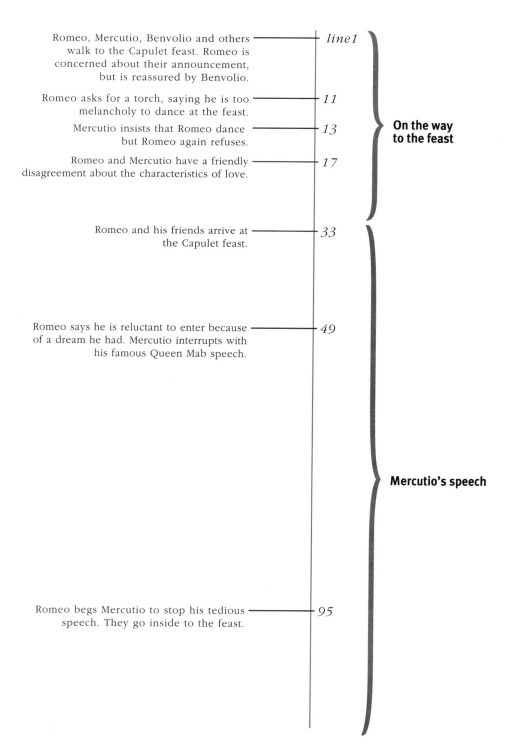

Romeo, Mercutio, Benvolio and others walk to the Capulet feast. Romeo is concerned about their announcement, but is reassured by Benvolio. — *line 1*

Romeo asks for a torch, saying he is too melancholy to dance at the feast. — *11*

Mercutio insists that Romeo dance but Romeo again refuses. — *13*

Romeo and Mercutio have a friendly disagreement about the characteristics of love. — *17*

On the way to the feast

Romeo and his friends arrive at the Capulet feast. — *33*

Romeo says he is reluctant to enter because of a dream he had. Mercutio interrupts with his famous Queen Mab speech. — *49*

Mercutio's speech

Romeo begs Mercutio to stop his tedious speech. They go inside to the feast. — *95*

1.5

The servants bicker {

line 1 — Inside the Capulet house, two servants complain about their lack of help from the other servants.

15 — Capulet welcomes Romeo and his friends with assurances that the ladies will dance with them.

40 — Romeo sees Juliet for the first time and denies ever having been in love before.

52 — Tybalt recognizes Romeo's voice and calls for his rapier.

Romeo and Juliet meet {

63 — Capulet demands that Tybalt calm down, saying Romeo has a good reputation in Verona.

91 — Romeo approaches Juliet. They speak for the first time in sonnet form and share their first kiss.

108 — The Nurse calls to Juliet, saying her mother would like to speak with her. Romeo learns from the Nurse that Juliet is a Capulet.

118 — Romeo and his friends leave the feast.

The feast ends {

133 — Juliet discovers from the Nurse that Romeo is a Montague.

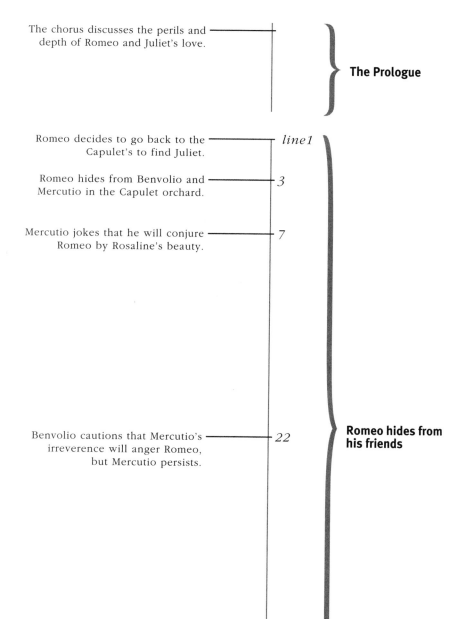

The chorus discusses the perils and depth of Romeo and Juliet's love.

The Prologue

Romeo decides to go back to the Capulet's to find Juliet. — *line1*

Romeo hides from Benvolio and Mercutio in the Capulet orchard. — *3*

Mercutio jokes that he will conjure Romeo by Rosaline's beauty. — *7*

Benvolio cautions that Mercutio's irreverence will anger Romeo, but Mercutio persists. — *22*

Romeo hides from his friends

Benvolio concludes that Romeo does not want to be found. He and Mercutio continue home. — *41*

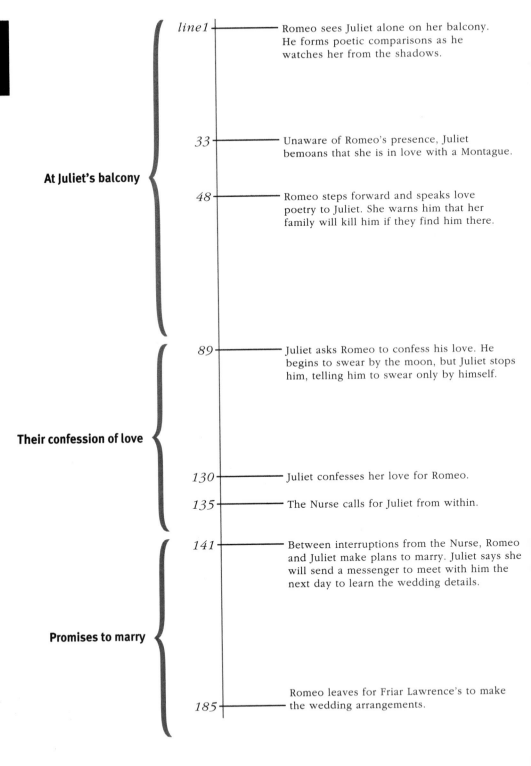

line 1 — Romeo sees Juliet alone on her balcony. He forms poetic comparisons as he watches her from the shadows.

33 — Unaware of Romeo's presence, Juliet bemoans that she is in love with a Montague.

At Juliet's balcony

48 — Romeo steps forward and speaks love poetry to Juliet. She warns him that her family will kill him if they find him there.

89 — Juliet asks Romeo to confess his love. He begins to swear by the moon, but Juliet stops him, telling him to swear only by himself.

Their confession of love

130 — Juliet confesses her love for Romeo.

135 — The Nurse calls for Juliet from within.

141 — Between interruptions from the Nurse, Romeo and Juliet make plans to marry. Juliet says she will send a messenger to meet with him the next day to learn the wedding details.

Promises to marry

185 — Romeo leaves for Friar Lawrence's to make the wedding arrangements.

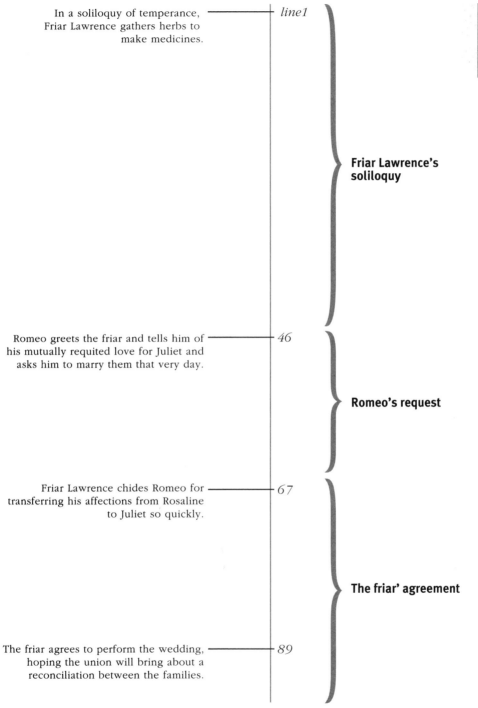

In a soliloquy of temperance, Friar Lawrence gathers herbs to make medicines. — *line1*

Friar Lawrence's soliloquy

Romeo greets the friar and tells him of his mutually requited love for Juliet and asks him to marry them that very day. — *46*

Romeo's request

Friar Lawrence chides Romeo for transferring his affections from Rosaline to Juliet so quickly. — *67*

The friar' agreement

The friar agrees to perform the wedding, hoping the union will bring about a reconciliation between the families. — *89*

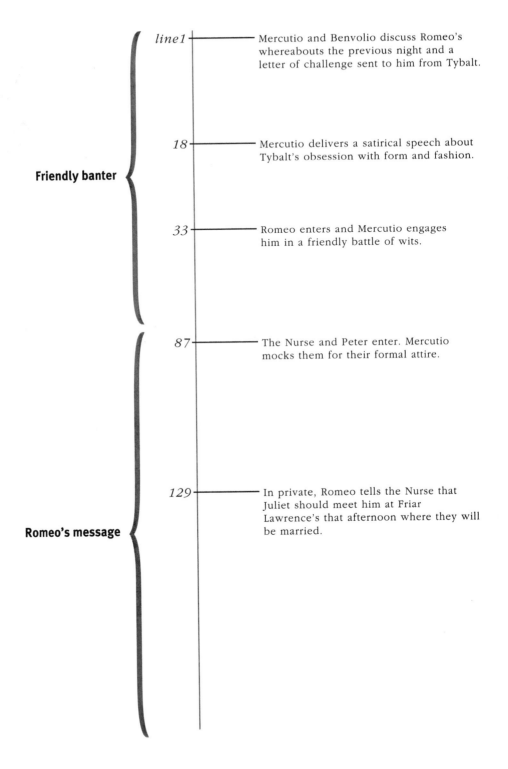

2.4

Friendly banter

line 1 — Mercutio and Benvolio discuss Romeo's whereabouts the previous night and a letter of challenge sent to him from Tybalt.

18 — Mercutio delivers a satirical speech about Tybalt's obsession with form and fashion.

33 — Romeo enters and Mercutio engages him in a friendly battle of wits.

87 — The Nurse and Peter enter. Mercutio mocks them for their formal attire.

Romeo's message

129 — In private, Romeo tells the Nurse that Juliet should meet him at Friar Lawrence's that afternoon where they will be married.

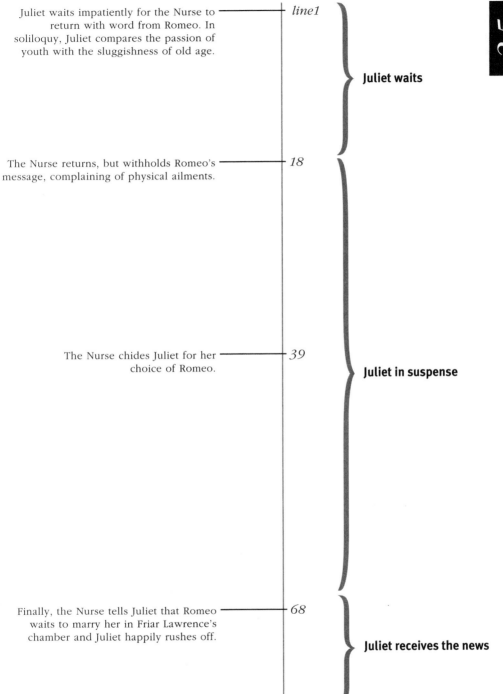

Juliet waits impatiently for the Nurse to
return with word from Romeo. In
soliloquy, Juliet compares the passion of
youth with the sluggishness of old age.

line 1

Juliet waits

The Nurse returns, but withholds Romeo's
message, complaining of physical ailments.

18

The Nurse chides Juliet for her
choice of Romeo.

39

Juliet in suspense

Finally, the Nurse tells Juliet that Romeo
waits to marry her in Friar Lawrence's
chamber and Juliet happily rushes off.

68

Juliet receives the news

2.5

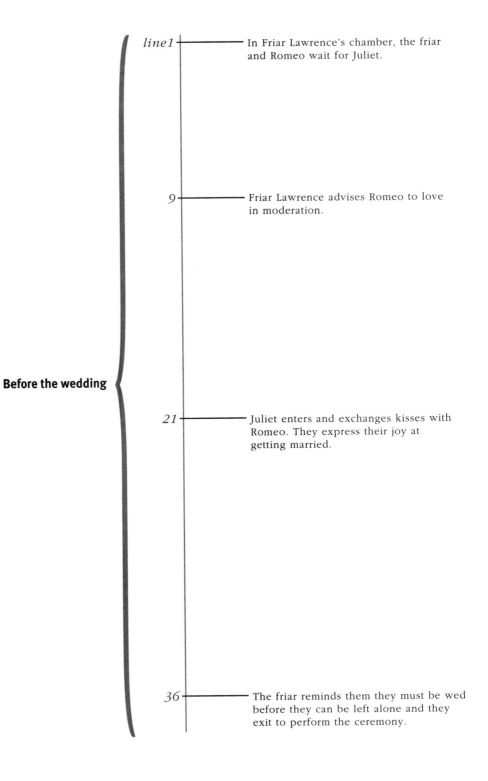

2.6

Before the wedding

line1 — In Friar Lawrence's chamber, the friar and Romeo wait for Juliet.

9 — Friar Lawrence advises Romeo to love in moderation.

21 — Juliet enters and exchanges kisses with Romeo. They express their joy at getting married.

36 — The friar reminds them they must be wed before they can be left alone and they exit to perform the ceremony.

Benvolio urges Mercutio to go inside to avoid a fight with the Capulets. — *line1*

Mercutio teases Benvolio. — *5*

Tybalt approaches, looking for Romeo. — *32*

Mercutio goads Tybalt for a fight. — *36*

Benvolio entreats them to discuss their differences in private. — *46*

Romeo enters and Tybalt insults him. — *52*

Romeo replies lovingly to Tybalt's insult — *58*

Mercutio is enraged by Romeo's passive response and draws is sword. — *69*

Mercutio and Tybalt fight. Tybalt mortally wounds Mercutio. — *80*

Mercutio dies. — *112*

Tybalt slays Mercutio

Romeo and Tybalt fight. Romeo kills Tybalt. — *127*

Romeo slays Tybalt

After hearing Benvolio's account of the fighting, the prince banishes Romeo. — *182*

Romeo is banished

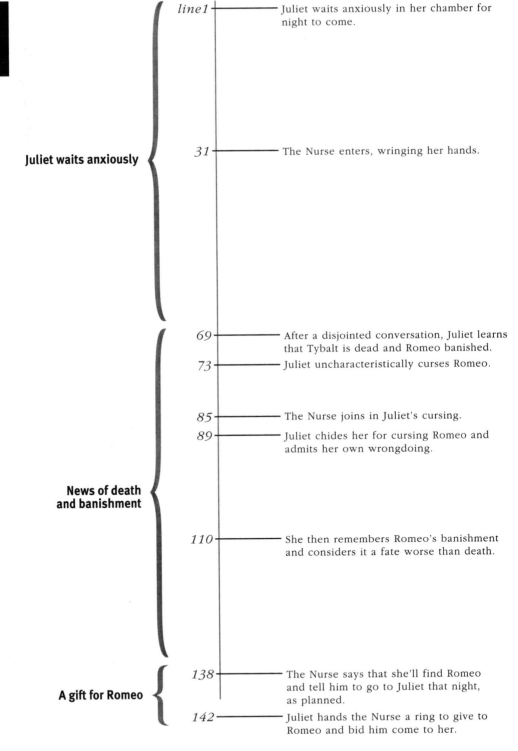

3.2

Juliet waits anxiously

line 1 — Juliet waits anxiously in her chamber for night to come.

31 — The Nurse enters, wringing her hands.

News of death and banishment

69 — After a disjointed conversation, Juliet learns that Tybalt is dead and Romeo banished.

73 — Juliet uncharacteristically curses Romeo.

85 — The Nurse joins in Juliet's cursing.

89 — Juliet chides her for cursing Romeo and admits her own wrongdoing.

110 — She then remembers Romeo's banishment and considers it a fate worse than death.

A gift for Romeo

138 — The Nurse says that she'll find Romeo and tell him to go to Juliet that night, as planned.

142 — Juliet hands the Nurse a ring to give to Romeo and bid him come to her.

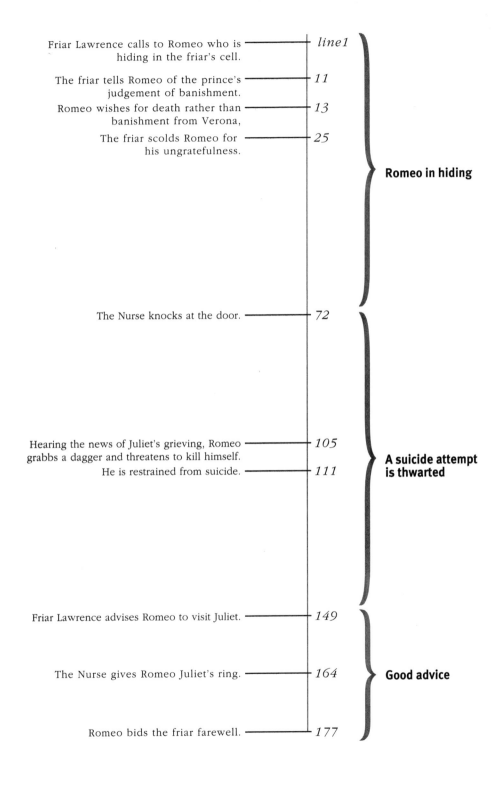

Friar Lawrence calls to Romeo who is hiding in the friar's cell. ———— *line1*

The friar tells Romeo of the prince's judgement of banishment. ———— *11*

Romeo wishes for death rather than banishment from Verona, ———— *13*

The friar scolds Romeo for his ungratefulness. ———— *25*

Romeo in hiding

The Nurse knocks at the door. ———— *72*

Hearing the news of Juliet's grieving, Romeo grabbs a dagger and threatens to kill himself. ———— *105*

He is restrained from suicide. ———— *111*

A suicide attempt is thwarted

Friar Lawrence advises Romeo to visit Juliet. ———— *149*

The Nurse gives Romeo Juliet's ring. ———— *164*

Good advice

Romeo bids the friar farewell. ———— *177*

3.3

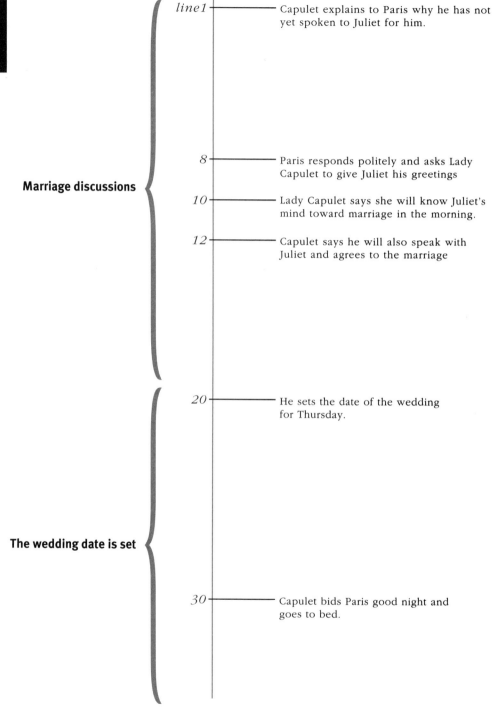

3.4

line 1 — Capulet explains to Paris why he has not yet spoken to Juliet for him.

Marriage discussions

8 — Paris responds politely and asks Lady Capulet to give Juliet his greetings

10 — Lady Capulet says she will know Juliet's mind toward marriage in the morning.

12 — Capulet says he will also speak with Juliet and agrees to the marriage

20 — He sets the date of the wedding for Thursday.

The wedding date is set

30 — Capulet bids Paris good night and goes to bed.

In Juliet's bedroom, she tries to convince ———— *line1*
Romeo that it is not yet time for him to go.

He tells her that it is morning and he ———— *6*
must go to avoid being killed.

Juliet continues pleading with him to stay. ———— *12*

Romeo resigns himself to death for her sake. ———— *17*

Juliet then tells him that he must go. ———— *26*

The Aubade

The Nurse enters and tells Juliet ———— *37*
her mother is coming

Romeo and Juliet part among ———— *41*
premonitions of death.

Lady Capulet enters and scolds Juliet for ———— *69*
excessive grieving for Tybalt.

Lady Capulet tells Juliet of the ———— *112*
wedding arrangements.

Juliet refuses to marry Paris. ———— *116*

Capulet enters and Lady Capulet tells ———— *126*
him of Juliet's decision.

Juliet's refusal

Capulet insults Juliet and threatens her ———— *149*
with disownment for her refusal.

The Nurse tries to intervene. ———— *168*

Juliet begs her mother for help ———— *199*
but she refuses.

When her parents have gone, Juliet turns ———— *205*
to the Nurse for help.

The Nurse advises Juliet to forget about ———— *213*
Romeo and marry Paris.

Alone, Juliet resolves to seek help from ———— *236*
Friar Lawrence.

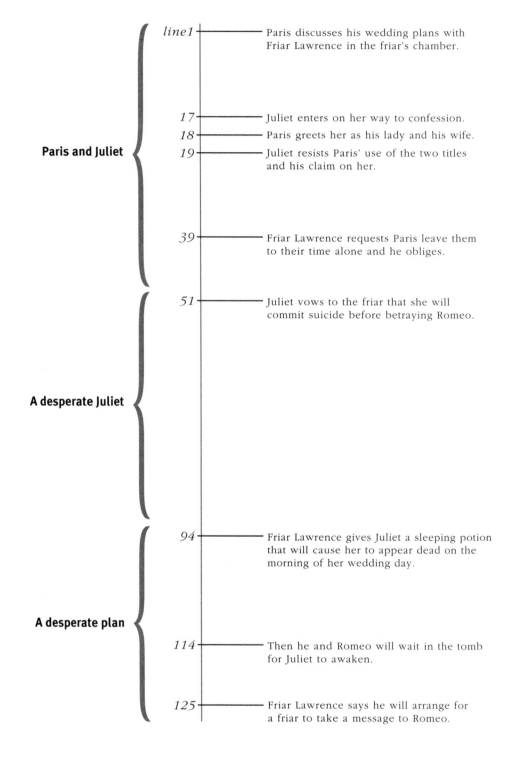

4.1

Paris and Juliet

line 1 — Paris discusses his wedding plans with Friar Lawrence in the friar's chamber.

17 — Juliet enters on her way to confession.
18 — Paris greets her as his lady and his wife.
19 — Juliet resists Paris' use of the two titles and his claim on her.

39 — Friar Lawrence requests Paris leave them to their time alone and he obliges.

A desperate Juliet

51 — Juliet vows to the friar that she will commit suicide before betraying Romeo.

A desperate plan

94 — Friar Lawrence gives Juliet a sleeping potion that will cause her to appear dead on the morning of her wedding day.

114 — Then he and Romeo will wait in the tomb for Juliet to awaken.

125 — Friar Lawrence says he will arrange for a friar to take a message to Romeo.

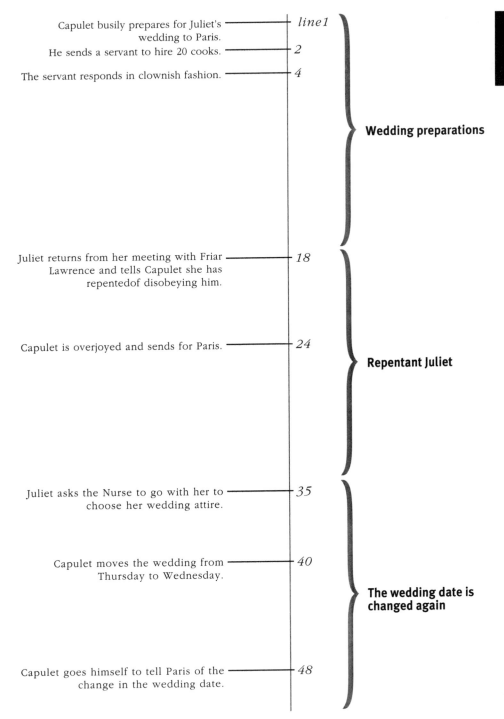

Capulet busily prepares for Juliet's wedding to Paris. — *line1*

He sends a servant to hire 20 cooks. — *2*

The servant responds in clownish fashion. — *4*

Wedding preparations

Juliet returns from her meeting with Friar Lawrence and tells Capulet she has repentedof disobeying him. — *18*

Capulet is overjoyed and sends for Paris. — *24*

Repentant Juliet

Juliet asks the Nurse to go with her to choose her wedding attire. — *35*

Capulet moves the wedding from Thursday to Wednesday. — *40*

The wedding date is changed again

Capulet goes himself to tell Paris of the change in the wedding date. — *48*

4.2

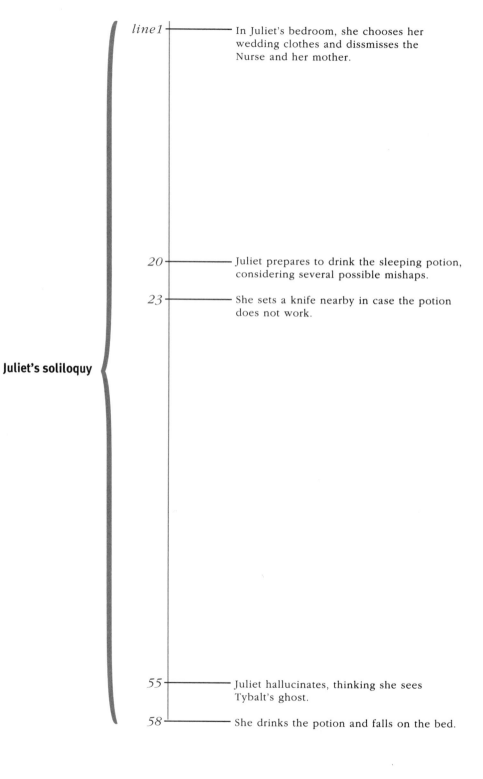

4.3

line 1 — In Juliet's bedroom, she chooses her wedding clothes and dissmisses the Nurse and her mother.

20 — Juliet prepares to drink the sleeping potion, considering several possible mishaps.

23 — She sets a knife nearby in case the potion does not work.

Juliet's soliloquy

55 — Juliet hallucinates, thinking she sees Tybalt's ghost.

58 — She drinks the potion and falls on the bed.

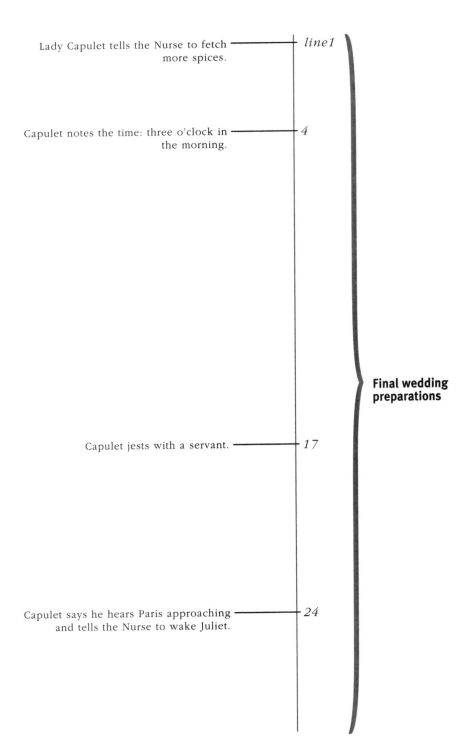

Lady Capulet tells the Nurse to fetch more spices. —— *line1*

Capulet notes the time: three o'clock in the morning. —— *4*

Capulet jests with a servant. —— *17*

Capulet says he hears Paris approaching and tells the Nurse to wake Juliet. —— *24*

Final wedding preparations

4.4

4.5

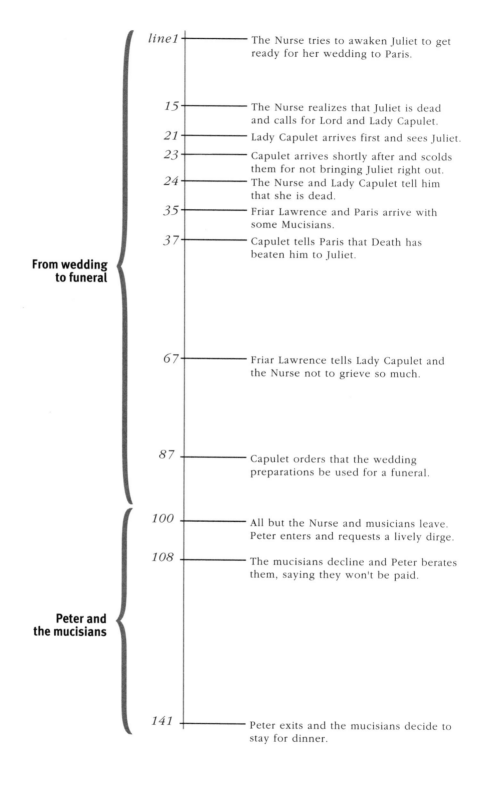

line 1 — The Nurse tries to awaken Juliet to get ready for her wedding to Paris.

15 — The Nurse realizes that Juliet is dead and calls for Lord and Lady Capulet.

21 — Lady Capulet arrives first and sees Juliet.

23 — Capulet arrives shortly after and scolds them for not bringing Juliet right out.

24 — The Nurse and Lady Capulet tell him that she is dead.

35 — Friar Lawrence and Paris arrive with some Mucisians.

37 — Capulet tells Paris that Death has beaten him to Juliet.

From wedding to funeral

67 — Friar Lawrence tells Lady Capulet and the Nurse not to grieve so much.

87 — Capulet orders that the wedding preparations be used for a funeral.

100 — All but the Nurse and musicians leave. Peter enters and requests a lively dirge.

108 — The mucisians decline and Peter berates them, saying they won't be paid.

Peter and the mucisians

141 — Peter exits and the mucisians decide to stay for dinner.

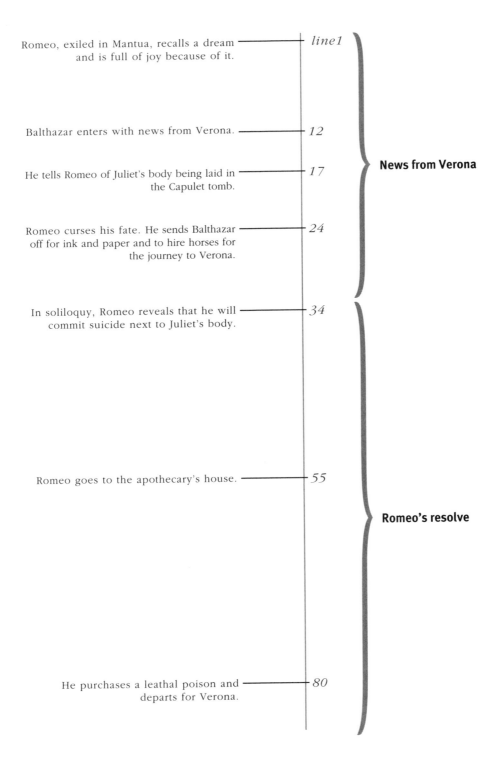

Romeo, exiled in Mantua, recalls a dream ————— *line1*
and is full of joy because of it.

Balthazar enters with news from Verona. ————— *12*

He tells Romeo of Juliet's body being laid in ————— *17*
the Capulet tomb.

News from Verona

Romeo curses his fate. He sends Balthazar ————— *24*
off for ink and paper and to hire horses for
the journey to Verona.

In soliloquy, Romeo reveals that he will ————— *34*
commit suicide next to Juliet's body.

Romeo goes to the apothecary's house. ————— *55*

Romeo's resolve

He purchases a leathal poison and ————— *80*
departs for Verona.

5.1

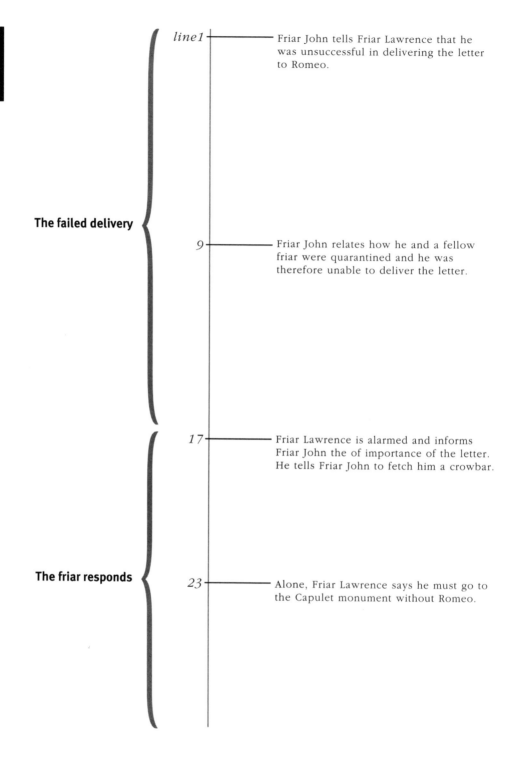

The failed delivery

line 1 — Friar John tells Friar Lawrence that he was unsuccessful in delivering the letter to Romeo.

9 — Friar John relates how he and a fellow friar were quarantined and he was therefore unable to deliver the letter.

17 — Friar Lawrence is alarmed and informs Friar John the of importance of the letter. He tells Friar John to fetch him a crowbar.

The friar responds

23 — Alone, Friar Lawrence says he must go to the Capulet monument without Romeo.

At the Capulet tomb, Paris tells his ——— *line1*
page to keep watch.

Paris strews flowers over the tomb. ——— *12*

The page warns Paris, and he hides as ——— *18*
Romeo and Balthazar approach.

Romeo sends Blathazar away with a letter to ——— *22*
his father. Instead Balthazar hides nearby.

Paris grieves

Romeo curses the tomb as he forces it open. ——— *45*

Paris steps forward to arrest Romeo. ——— *55*

Paris and Romeo fight and Paris falls. As ——— *71*
he dies, he asks to be laid with Juliet.

Romeo agrees, then recognizes him as ——— *74*
Paris who was to marry Juliet.

The death of Romeo

Seeing Juliet, Romeo remarks that Death ——— *91*
has not marred her beauty.

Romeo promises to remain with Juliet in ——— *106*
the tomb forever.

He takes a final embrace, drinks the ——— *113*
poison and dies.

Friar Lawrence arrives at the churchyard ——— *121*
and finds out Romeo has been there.

Juliet awakens

The friar enters the tomb and discovers ——— *140*
Romeo and Paris dead.

Juliet awakes ——— *147*

Friar Lawrence tries to convince her to ——— *151*
leave the tomb with him, pointing out
that Romeo and Paris are dead.

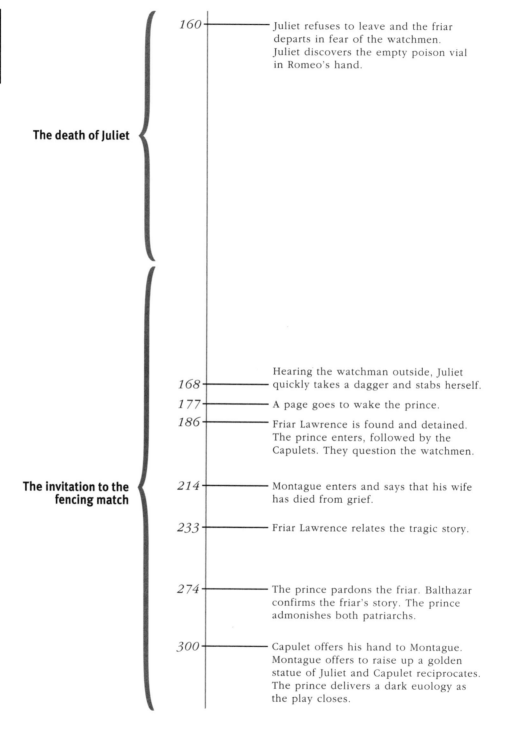

The death of Juliet

160 — Juliet refuses to leave and the friar departs in fear of the watchmen. Juliet discovers the empty poison vial in Romeo's hand.

The invitation to the fencing match

168 — Hearing the watchman outside, Juliet quickly takes a dagger and stabs herself.

177 — A page goes to wake the prince.

186 — Friar Lawrence is found and detained. The prince enters, followed by the Capulets. They question the watchmen.

214 — Montague enters and says that his wife has died from grief.

233 — Friar Lawrence relates the tragic story.

274 — The prince pardons the friar. Balthazar confirms the friar's story. The prince admonishes both patriarchs.

300 — Capulet offers his hand to Montague. Montague offers to raise up a golden statue of Juliet and Capulet reciprocates. The prince delivers a dark euology as the play closes.

APPENDIX B: BACKGROUND

After careful thought we decided to place the background material—generally the first information you see—at the end of the guidebook. The two most compelling reasons for doing so were, first, we did not want to lose the powerful beginning of the opening chapter ("This is Juliet"); and, second, it has been our experience that the background material is usually passed over and then read last anyway. Having said this, we feel that the material in Appendix B is extremely useful to the reader wishing an expanded view of Shakespeare's life as well as sources and nuance relating to *Romeo and Juliet*.

Shakespeare achieved success in his lifetime.

BUSINESSMAN. Born in 1564—the same year as Galileo—by the time William Shakespeare was 28, he had settled in London as an actor. At 30, he became a shareholder in the Lord Chamberlain's Men, a successful company who often staged plays at court for Queen Elizabeth I.

ACTOR. Shakespeare began as a player and part-time playwright, later focusing all of his energies on writing. He mostly acted character parts—not leading roles—although he is known to have played the character of Old Hamlet's ghost. He received far more income from his acting than from his writing royalties.

PLAYWRIGHT. He is widely regarded as the greatest dramatist of western literature and by some as the greatest thinker. Shakespeare's plays, replete with insights into human character, are performed more often than any other playwright's in history. He achieved success in his own lifetime and, by the time his wife died in 1623, a monument to Shakespeare had been erected in Holy Trinity Church in their hometown of Stratford.

Romeo and Juliet has mythological roots.

MISGUIDED DOUBLE SUICIDE: *PYRAMUS AND THISBE*

The story of Pyramus and Thisbe is found in the masterwork *Metamorphoses,* a first century collection of myth written by the Roman poet Ovid. Forbidden by their parents to see each other, Pyramus and Thisbe agree to meet in the forest. Thisbe arrives first, but is chased away by a lion, who manages to rip her scarf. Pyramus finds the scarf and, thinking his love is dead, kills himself. Thisbe returns to find the dying Pyramus and kills herself with his sword.

LOVE AGAINST PARENTAL WISHES: *CUPID AND PSYCHE*

Lucius Apuleius' second century myth tells the story of Cupid, who disobeys his mother Venus by coming to Psyche at night, unseen. Psyche eventually views her lover by the light of a hidden oil lamp, but accidentally burns Cupid as he flees. To find Cupid, Psyche completes several impossible tasks given her by Venus. After the final task, Psyche falls into a slumber and awakens, transformed into a goddess. She and Cupid marry.

THE SLEEPING POTION ENTOMBMENT: *EPHESIACA*

The second century Greek writer, Xenophon of Ephesus, creates the early prototypes to Juliet and Romeo—Anthia and Habrocomes. His story contains a sleeping potion Anthia takes to thwart an arranged marriage, misguided news reaching the ears of her true love, and her true love's first reaction to kill himself.

1. *Novella* by Masuccio Salernitano

In Siena, Mariotto Mignanelli and Giannozza Saracini bribe a friar to marry them in secret (no motive is given for the secrecy). Mariotto accidentally kills a prominent citizen and is exiled to Alexandria. After sending word to Mariotto, Giannozza takes a sleeping potion procured from the friar to avoid marrying a man of her father's choosing. Buried by her family, she is freed by the friar and promptly sails to Alexandria. Fatefully, pirates murder the messenger sent to tell Mariotto of Giannozza's feigned death. When Mariotto hears of her death from his brother, he returns to Siena disguised as a pilgrim and attempts to open the tomb. He is arrested as a thief, recognized as the banished Mariotto and beheaded. Giannozza returns home and dies in a convent. There is no mention of feuding families and the lovers do not commit suicide.

2. *A Newfound Story of Two Noble Lovers* by Luigi da Porto

The story is set in Verona with the feuding Montecchi and the Cappelletti families. Romeo, disguised as a nymph, attends a Carnival ball held at the Cappelletti house. There, he searches for an unnamed girl who spurns his affections. Instead, he meets Giulietta, who is seeking relief from Marcuccio's cold hands, and quickly forgets about his unrequited love. Giulietta discovers Romeo is a Montecchi, but believes their union may end the strife between the families. The two see each other at church and Romeo often visits her chamber window at night. On one such visit, it is snowing, so Romeo begs admittance to Giulietta's room. The two agree to marry in secret and Friar Lorenzo performs the ceremony—believing like Giulietta that it may end the hostility between the families. Afterward, Romeo kills Thebaldo Cappelletti, Giulietta's cousin, in a street fight arising from the senseless feud. Romeo is banished and Friar Lorenzo arranges a final farewell between the two, before helping the fugitive Romeo's flight to Mantua. In a marriage arranged by her father, Giulietta is promised to Conte di Lodrone (introducing the title of count). She procures a sleeping potion from the friar and drinks it the night before her wedding. Giulietta's feigned death is reported as true to Romeo while he is in Mantua. Seeing her in the tomb, Romeo mistakes Giulietta's sleep for death and kills himself. When Giulietta wakes, she kills herself by holding her breath. The governor dispenses justice at the end and the two families reconcile.

3. *Giulietta and Romeo* by Matteo Bandello

In Bandello's version, Romeo's initial love-melancholy is emphasized. Romeo attends the ball in a masque with several other young gentlemen. He is recognized when he removes his mask, but appears so young and handsome that no one insults him. Giulietta is 18 years old. Mercutio, who has a minor role, is described as a libertine. The prototype of the Nurse is introduced as a minor character, although she shares similarities with Shakespeare's Benvolio. Romeo learns Giulietta's identity from a friend as he leaves the ball. Giulietta finds out who Romeo is from the Nurse. Giulietta wants to run off with the banished Romeo, but he forbids it. When he learns the false news that Giulietta is dead, Romeo writes a letter to his father explaining everything. Giulietta and Romeo share a scene in the tomb where they are both alive: Giulietta awakens in the tomb, at first alarmed at Romeo's disguised figure and she fears the Friar has betrayed her; she soon recognizes Romeo and the lovers mutually lament their misfortune; Romeo regrets killing Tibaldo and urges Giulietta to live on after his own death; Giulietta will not listen and she kills herself by holding her breath.

4. *Tragic Histories* by Pierre Boiastuau

For the first time, the names Romeo and Juliet are used in the story. Romeo attends the ball hoping he will find a new woman to help him forget about his unrequited love. Juliet's father loses his temper with Juliet for not wanting to marry Paris, introducing the power of the patriarchal system. Also, Romeo dies before Juliet awakens and she kills herself with Romeo's dagger. The Friar explains the whole situation to prove his innocence, the apothecary is hanged and the Nurse is banished for concealing the marriage.

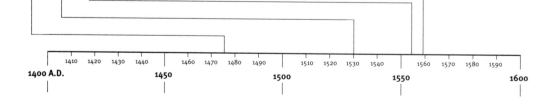

| 1400 A.D. | 1410 | 1420 | 1430 | 1440 | 1450 | 1460 | 1470 | 1480 | 1490 | 1500 | 1510 | 1520 | 1530 | 1540 | 1550 | 1560 | 1570 | 1580 | 1590 | 1600 |

Romeo and Juliet's Renaissance sources.

TRANSITIONAL STORY: *SALERNITANO,* 1476

As the Medieval Age was making the transformation into the European Renaissance, the fragment of the Ephesiaca myth containing the sleeping potion transformed into a story more closely resembling what we now recognize as Romeo and Juliet. The friar and the banishment are introduced.

A FAMILIAR STORY TAKES SHAPE: *DA PORTO,* 1530.

Among the familiar elements introduced by da Porto are Verona, the feud, aristocratic backgrounds, the prototype to Rosaline, Mercutio's prototype, Mantua, the all-important double suicide and the reconciliation of the families.

PATRIARCHY AND MORALIZING: *BANDELLO,* 1554.

Italian writer Matteo Bandello wrote a version in 1554 in his collection of over 200 short stories, called *Il Novellio.* The Nurse prototype is introduced and Conte Lodrone is first called Paris. In his version, Bandello places a high premium on the social force that stabilize the patriarchy and includes a moralizing admonition to temperate living.

SOCIAL DISORDER: *BOAISTAU,* 1559.

Boaistau paints Verona as a dystopic society on the verge of social collapse. The destitute apothecary is introduced. The deaths of the lovers are the only events capable of bringing the final reconciliation.

1. *The Tragicall Historye of Romeus and Juliet* by Arthur Brooke

After a moralizing preface, the feud is assigned to mutual envy. Brooke includes: the unrequited infatuation; the meeting at the Capulet feast (a Christmas party in this version); the balcony love promises; the friar's hopes of ending the feud; the Nurse as liaison; a honeymoon; Tybalt's attacks (with a band of Capulets on Easter); Romeus' banishment; Romeus' shelter at the friar's and the Nurse's visit; Capulet's arrangements for Juliet to marry Paris, hoping it will end his daughter's supposed grief at the death of Tybalt; the friar's dubious sleeping potion strategy; Juliet's insincere repentance; the mock burial; the bungled message; the misdirected news to Romeus; the apothecary; the death of Romeus (no encounter with Paris); Juliet's recovery as the friar flees from the watchmen; Juliet's suicide (she stabs herself); an open inquiry: the prince's dispensation of justice (the apothecary is hanged and the Nurse is banished); the reconciliation of the families; the monument to Romeus and Juliet. Fortune is held responsible throughout the play.

2. *The Palace of Pleasure* by William Painter

A faithful translation of Bandello. Painter takes a far less rational view of the action and adopts a more inquisitive attitude toward the amicable love between the protagonists. Painter's collection of stories was reprinted about a decade and a half before Shakespeare's masterpiece.

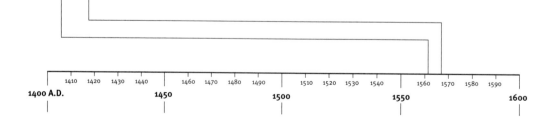

1400 A.D. 1410 1420 1430 1440 1450 1460 1470 1480 1490 1500 1510 1520 1530 1540 1550 1560 1570 1580 1590 1600

Shakespeare used two primary sources.

RATIONAL AND MORAL CHARACTER: *BROOKE,* 1562

Arthur Brooke's poem *The Tragicall Historye of Romeus and Juliet,* published two years before Shakespeare's birth, was based on Boaistuau. Brooke's poem emphasizes the workings of Fortune in the lives of the lovers. He also begins with a moral exemplum—echoing Bandello—and his characters adopt a logical thought process to work through their problems. The raw material for the story is intact, however, and it is thought that Shakespeare used Brooke as his primary source. By way of departure from Brooke, Shakespeare compressed the duration of events from nine months to less than a week (Brooke's Romeus and Juliet are married for three months before Tybalt is slain); at 13 years old, Shakespeare's Juliet is three years younger than Brooke's; and Shakespeare masterfully fashioned the charismatic Mercutio from just a few lines of his source.

THE CLOSEST SOURCE: *PAINTER,* 1567.

A little less than three decades prior to Shakespeare's drama, William Painter published a translation of Boaistuau's story in his collection, *The Palace of Pleasure.* Painter's translation, more faithful to Boaistuau than Brooke, was republished in 1580.

The Death of Mercutio

Wishing to continue his grievance, Tybalt challenges Romeo, who responds peaceably. Mercutio accepts for him and Tybalt kills Mercutio. Enraged, Romeo kills Tybalt and is banished by the prince.

part 1: comedy

turning point

part 2: tragedy

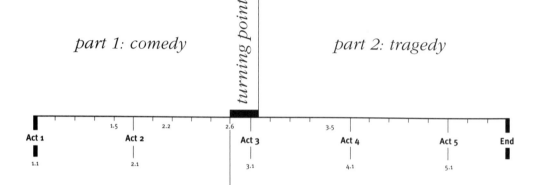

	1.5	2.2	2.6		3.5				
Act 1	Act 2		Act 3		Act 4		Act 5		End
1.1	2.1		3.1		4.1		5.1		

The Wedding of Romeo and Juliet

Friar Lawrence marries Romeo and Juliet in hopes that their union will end the destructive feud between the two families.

Part 1: Before the wedding	Part 2: After the death of Mercutio
There are incompetent clowns	There are concerned pages
There is a feast	There is a mock funeral
There is a request for dancing	There is a request for a dirge
There are vows of love	There are resolutions to die
Juliet is compared to the sun	Romeo is compared to a dead man
Capulet considers Juliet's feelings	Capulet disregards Juliet's feelings
Tybalt is restrained	Tybalt is unrestricted
Mercutio is witty	Mercutio is dead
The friar is optimistic	The friar is desperate
Options multiply	Options diminish
Ends in a secret wedding	Ends in a double suicide

Romeo and Juliet is an unusual tragedy.

VICTIMS. A typical tragedy is about heroes—a suffering fall of a king or person of high station—not about two kids. Usually the protagonist contains a character trait that is the catalyst for his or her own fall. Romeo and Juliet, in contrast, are undeserving of their fate. They are victimized by their families, by the feud, by the violence around them: they are not morally culpable. Distinct from a heroic tragedy, *Romeo and Juliet* is a tragedy of pathos, exploiting the protagonists' youth and inexperience.

COMEDY. Comedies typically open with clowns. *Romeo and Juliet* opens with the clown-like exchange between Sampson and Gregory. Comedies typically enjoy a festive mood—parties, music, love poetry. *Romeo and Juliet* manifests these elements before act one is over. Comedies typically highlight a character who embodies the comic spirit, one who is bawdy, earthy, witty, extroverted. *Romeo and Juliet* has such a character in Mercutio—and then he is killed! Upon the death of Mercutio the comic potential is extinguished, and the play develops organically into a tragedy, with a decreasing number of options and a gathering set of consequences.